THE FAST FACILITATOR

76 Reproducible Facilitator Activities and Interventions Covering
Essential Skills, Group Processes, and Creative Techniques

Anthony Landale
Mica Douglas

HRD Press, Inc. • Amherst • Massachusetts

Published by: HRD Press, Inc.
                22 Amherst Road
                Amherst, Massachusetts 01002
                1-800-822-2801 (U.S. and Canada)
                1-413-253-3488
                1-413-253-3490 (fax)
                http://www.hrdpress.com

ISBN: 978-1-61014-384-4

Editorial services by Suzanne Bay and Sally Farnham
Production services by Anctil Virtual Office
Cover design by Eileen Klockars

Contents

Key Issues: A Quick Guide

Attentiveness

One of the core skills in facilitation is to be acutely attentive. This is more than just active listening—it's about knowing when and how to ask questions, how to observe accurately, and how to pick up on nonverbal cues.

Facilitator option: Read Section 2.6, including Activity 38, and Section 3.3.

Beginnings and Endings

Developing your awareness of how to begin and end meetings, training events, ongoing groups, and team briefings is an important part of creating trust and achieving the task.

Facilitator option: Read Sections 1.4 and 3.10.

Coaching

Facilitators need to know how to work effectively on a one-to-one level as well as in groups and teams in order to encourage and empower staff members and solve problems.

Facilitator option: The theory and activities in Section 3.1 provide an introduction to this skill area. There are also activities in every section relating to coaching.

Collusion

You may sometimes find yourself colluding with team or group members, or you may notice the group or team as a whole colluding to avoid an issue. To deal with this, you need sensitivity and clarity.

Facilitator option: Read Section 2.8 on scapegoating, which discusses the sensitive handling of issues that groups tend to avoid.

Communication

A great many of the facilitation skills are about clear and assertive communication with individual employees, teams, and customers.

Facilitator option: See Section 2.9 on negotiation skills, which focuses on the individual and group skills you will need to achieve win–win outcomes. Look at Sections 1.6 and 1.10 for specific communication techniques. For more information on nonverbal communication, read Section 3.3.

Creative Facilitation

The beauty of facilitation is that there is no one right way to manage or develop others. It is important to develop your own personal facilitation style and unique skills.

Facilitator option: See Section 1.2 on the qualities of facilitation; Section 1.3 on self-awareness; and Sections 3.7 and 3.8 on creative facilitation.

Culture

How do you establish a team or working culture that encourages people to be fully involved and supported? This is an ongoing challenge for facilitators. It requires an understanding of facilitator authority, group development, and authentic leadership.

Facilitator option: Read Section 1.6 on contracting; Section 1.7 on valuing; and Sections 2.1, 2.2 and 2.3 on the issues of inclusion, control, and openness. See Activity 69, an interesting exercise that looks at organizational culture.

Emotional Expression

Outbursts of emotion can be disconcerting in work settings. However, skillful facilitators should be trying to help their teams and staff express their emotions appropriately. The question is how best to do this.

Facilitator option: You will need to know how to shut down destructive behavior, as well as how to encourage people to express their feelings. See Section 1.8 on managing feelings and Section 1.7 on valuing ideas. Activity 44 is a useful activity for helping groups examine the subject of emotions.

Feedback

Giving positive, constructive, and challenging feedback is one of the ways a facilitator establishes a learning culture and builds trust among teams and groups. It is a key tool in the facilitator's toolkit.

Facilitator option: Section 1.10 focuses on how to give and receive feedback. Section 2.10 focuses on the need for facilitators to get feedback from their own peers as part of their own continuous development.

Fight/Flight

Defense mechanisms such as fight/flight can be triggered in a moment, and usually involve a reduction in participation levels and trust. Facilitators need to understand how such a simple defense mechanism is triggered and what to do about it when it occurs.

Facilitator option: Read Section 1.9 on challenging behavior; Section 2.8 on scapegoating; and Section 3.4 on defense patterns.

Focusing

When a team or group loses focus, people will quickly become frustrated and demotivated. In these circumstances the facilitator needs to take charge and reestablish aims, objectives, and perspective.

Facilitator option: Making sure that people are clear about the task and process is one of the issues here (see Section 1.1). You will also need to know how and when to intervene (see Section 2.6). Section 1.5 on the need for planning is also relevant, and Activity 71 is a good exercise for helping teams see where they have reached in relation to their objective.

Group Behavior

As a facilitator, you will need some understanding of the ways in which groups behave and develop.

Facilitator option: Sections 2.1, 2.2, 2.3, and 2.4 provide the facilitator with some of the key dynamics involved in group behavior.

Leadership

Facilitators need to be able to use different leadership styles and ways of using authority and power so that they can respond appropriately to different teams and different requirements.

Facilitator option: See Section 2.5 for a discussion of different styles of leadership and when each is most useful.

Motivation

Lack of motivation from group members (who either do not want to be present or are cynical about the company, the meeting, or the project in which they are engaged) makes facilitation hard work. So how do you tackle resistance and cynicism before others become contaminated with it, too?

Facilitator option: Read Section 1.8 on managing feelings and Section 1.9 on challenging behavior, which both address how to work with resistance.

Openness

There is a great need for transparency and openness in most aspects of today's society. This does not mean that we have to reveal everything about ourselves, but when people withhold information or knowledge at work that should be shared, it is a problem that needs to be addressed.

Facilitator option: The activities in Section 1.7 are worth looking at here, as are Section 2.2 on control and Section 2.3 on openness. How open we are to getting support from others is also worth considering (see Section 2.10).

Personal Presence and Self-Confidence

Some people know their facts, but when it comes to communicating with other people, they find it hard to put their message across. Others need to develop their personal authority.

Facilitator option: Read Sections 3.2 and 3.6. Activity 58 is also useful here.

Perspective

Sometimes people get locked in to viewing the world in only one way. Helping people break free of their filters is a way to help teams and groups appreciate one another's strengths and weaknesses and to see that there are many different ways to solve problems.

Facilitator option: Read Section 2.7 on diversity; Section 1.3 on self-awareness; and the activities in Sections 1.3, 1.4 and 3.6, which highlight the different ways in which we can relate to one another.

Power

When power struggles occur in teams and groups, you will need to look at role clarity, control, or status issues.

Facilitator option: See Section 2.7 and work through the power grid activity (Activity 42). Read Section 2.8 on scapegoating, which discusses abuse of power and ways to address it.

"Process" Roles

Identifying the roles that people occupy in teams and groups helps build relationships and trust in the group, and moves the process along.

Facilitator option: To identify these roles and identify which ones you are skilled at, see Section 2.4, which explains the positive and negative aspects of each.

Reactive Behavior

Reactive behavior is most easily seen when people lose perspective and act out their feelings of hurt, mistrust, and betrayal by getting into conflict, withdrawal, or resistance.

Facilitator option: Be aware that behavior breeds behavior; examine your own behavior first to see if you are causing this reaction somehow. See Section 1.3 on self-awareness, and read Section 1.9 to become familiar with flight/fight responses.

Resolving Conflict

When conflicts occur in groups, it is useful to have some facilitative strategies on hand that will help you deal with the situation, whether it is between you and a group member or between two fellow group members.

Facilitator option: The key to conflict resolution is knowing what you want and being able to hear what other people want. Once you understand other people's positions, it will be far easier to find solutions and common ground. See Section 1.9 on challenging behavior; Section 2.7 on diversity; and Section 3.4 on defense patterns. See also the activities in Section 2.9.

Skills Building

All facilitators need skills. Remember, however, that skills need to be built on self-awareness, or they will not be effective (see Section 1.3). There is a set of core skills that all facilitators should use (active listening, facilitative speaking, acute observation, and skillful questioning).

Facilitator option: Read Sections 2.6, 3.1, 3.3, and 3.6 and Activities 8, 16, and 58.

Stages of Groups

If you are working with ongoing teams, you will need to recognize each stage the group is going through and what to do to help the group through this process.

Facilitator option: The stages of group development are outlined in Sections 2.4 and 2.5.

Task Roles

Identifying the roles that people take in a group will help the group achieve the task effectively and efficiently.

Facilitator option: To identify these roles, see Section 2.1, which explains the positive and negative aspects of task roles. Activities 70 and 71 are also useful.

Teamwork

This is one of the main areas in facilitation, encompassing a broad spectrum of skills.

Facilitator option: Read about the way people, groups, and teams behave in Sections 2.1, 2.3, 2.4, and 2.5. Specific exercises that highlight team dynamics can be found in Sections 1.1, 2.1, 2.2, 3.8, and 3.9.

Trust

Facilitators who need to lead teams or empower others need to engender trust and create an environment of openness and support.

Facilitator option: Read Section 1.6 on contracting; Section 1.7 on valuing; and Section 3.1 on one-to-one facilitation. Section 2.10 on how you support yourself is also valuable. Activities 28 and 32 are also useful here.

Introduction

· ·

This resource manual for managers, trainers, and consultants deals with the skills of facilitation at the following levels:

- Essential Facilitation Skills
- Facilitation of Groups and Teams
- Creative Facilitation

Why facilitation?

Facilitation is an extremely significant aspect of management. The pressing challenge that many managers, consultants, and trainers face is how to harness potential and engender responsibility in individuals and teams so that targets can be reached and tasks achieved. Facilitation is an effective competency for this. It has a strong theoretical base, is grounded in people-centered values, and provides practical gateways for the manager to respond appropriately to the needs of individuals and businesses. Facilitation can help people learn, help people be more self-aware, encourage people to be more flexible in their thinking and behavior, and help people build their competence.

So how do people develop facilitation skills?

If you are a trainer, a manager, or a consultant, you will have developed and used some, or perhaps many, of the skills already. If so, you may simply be looking for practical and creative exercises that you can use with your people. These exercises are here—76 of them.

Facilitation, however, isn't always easy. We have tried to provide what you will need to know when using these exercises, such as background theory and suggestions for your own self-development. This is important: It is who you are and how well you know yourself that forms the backbone of facilitation. What we have tried to illustrate here is that facilitation is a coherent and distinctive approach to managing people that is effective, exhilarating, and creative. We hope this comes through in this manual.

The Approach

Use the manual when you want support in dealing with a specific issue at work or for professional skills development. Facilitation here is divided into three levels. Each chapter of the manual is organized into four distinct areas: theory, activities, coaching, and self-development.

1. *Theory*. Each topic is introduced by explaining the theory behind it, so the manager or trainer has a basis for his or her own understanding. We will highlight when to use the approach, models, or thinking that supports the activity, and give clear advice or guidance concerning the issue itself. This background in theory, with your own insights and experience, will help people make sense of the activity and/or the issues they are facing.

2. *Activities.* Several activities will be described for people who have some experience working with and training individuals, teams, or groups. Trainer guidance and suggestions are also provided.

   Note: We haven't adopted a rigorous menu-driven approach to the activities. Rather, we have given an outline of the activity and an approximation of the time you can expect each activity to take. However, much will depend on your style and the priority you give to the activity. You will need to decide how much time you have and how important the topic is, and adapt the material to your circumstances.

3. *Coaching.* In the coaching sections, we will explore how to facilitate on a one-to-one basis around the topic in question. This section is suitable for those consultants and managers who offer formal coaching and mentoring, as well as line managers or supervisors.

4. *Facilitator self-development.* There is a section at the end of each chapter that relates to the facilitator's own learning requirements. This will focus on what you need to consider and traps and difficulties you might encounter as a facilitator.

Materials and Duration of Activities

Most exercises call for flipchart paper and pens. Where more complex materials are required, we have indicated what these are. We also urge facilitators to use those resources that they have on hand, and not to be driven only by our suggestions. The time periods given here are approximate; much will depend on you and the readiness of the team or group. Be flexible and creative.

Acknowledgments

These exercises have come from a variety of experiences and sources. Many we have developed specifically for the individuals, groups, and teams with whom we have worked. Others grew out of training events we have participated in. We would especially like to acknowledge our own training in psychosynthesis, Gestalt, Transactional Analysis, and facilitation styles, which have promoted and inspired our own continuous personal and professional development.

Train the Facilitator

How you train others in facilitation will depend on your own skills and style. This manual and the outline below is not meant to be prescriptive, but it will guide you to the key issues and activities. It is then up to you to adapt to the needs of the people you are working with. Use their agenda and encourage them to practice facilitating.

With this in mind, here is a suggested Train the Facilitator program. There is a lot of ground to cover here, but if you can cover these issues, you will have built a practical foundation in facilitation skills.

Day 1: What is facilitation?

- Housekeeping, introductions, and structure
- Beginnings: Four-way meetings; mind, body, emotions, and belief (see Activity 8); why beginnings are important (see theory).
- Contracting: Introduction of theory and use of model of group effectiveness (see Activity 14).
- What is facilitation? Brainstorming with the team/group about what makes up the process aspect of the iceberg model (see Activity 2).
- What are the qualities of the facilitator? Introduction of theory and the body-mapping activity (see Activity 3).
- The need for self-awareness: Theory plus facilitated discussion (see Activity 5).
- Summing up: Update on where people are and what they have learned. Use Activity 64 to find out where people are at the end of the day.

Day 2: Key dimensions

- Facilitated opening discussion: Invite one of the group to facilitate a check-in to see what people have brought with them in terms of ideas, energy, problems, and understandings.
- Planning and structuring. See theory and Activity 12.
- Valuing. See theory and Activity 18.
- Managing feelings. See theory and Activity 19.
- A great deal of facilitation is about helping people make sense of what is going on. This is done by presenting theory, using models, offering insights, and telling stories. One of the key skills for facilitators is to make sure that people understand the issues that they are facing, so at this stage of the course, facilitate or ask one of the group to facilitate a discussion on how facilitators can build and promote understanding.

Day 3: Facilitator authority

- Facilitate opening discussion: Invite one of the group to facilitate a check-in to see what people have brought with them in terms of ideas, energy, problems, and understandings.
- Feedback: Introduce theory and then feedback review (see Activities 25 and 26).
- Challenging: Introduce theory and Activity 23.
- Introducing facilitator authority: Introduce theory and then Activity 30.
- Endings: Theory, plus final round of self- and peer-assessment (see Activity 73).

PART ONE

Essential Facilitation

1.1 What Is Facilitation?

Have you ever wished you had been taught differently? Have you ever sat through a meeting where nobody listened or nobody talked, or where the agenda was hijacked? Have you ever been part of a team where people didn't get on and where, consequently, morale was low and performance was suffering?

In these and many other situations, the skills of facilitation can be applied to great effect. Organizations are looking for ways to help their managers, trainers, and consultants become more effective; facilitation is now recognized as a core business skill.

Facilitation is about how something gets done, rather than what you do. In this sense, it is about the process as well as the task. The iceberg model shown below illustrates this difference: the top of the iceberg shows what is clear to all—the projects in which we are involved, the tasks we take on, the procedures that we abide by. It is what is conscious and visible. The submerged part of the iceberg, in contrast, contains our subconscious processes, which include our feelings, relationships, beliefs, fears, and prejudices. These processes aren't visible, but they are vital.

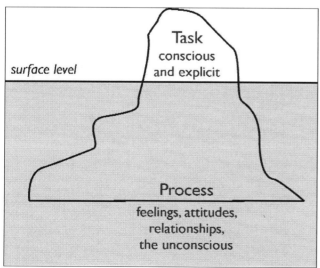

Iceberg Model

The facilitative manager, team leader, or consultant needs to keep both the task and the process in mind—the two cannot be separated. The business objective is to achieve the goal or performance that has been set, but unless the process is addressed along the way, the chances are that the objective may never be reached.

An example of this situation in practice is where there is a conflict within a team. Every team will be made up of people with different personalities, skills, ambitions, and views. The effective facilitator will be looking at ways to harness this diversity, but that is easier said than done. We have surely all been in teams where simmering resentment or frustration has been evident, but how many managers address these issues? And if they don't address them, what happens? Most conflicts don't just go away. It is up to the facilitator to be aware of these dynamics, to highlight them, and to help the participants involved to address them.

There is no set script for how the facilitator should address problems such as conflict. He or she might have to reestablish clear boundaries and contracts, or need to decide to find solutions in partnership with the individuals concerned. The way they decide to work will differ: one-to-one outside the team or group, with the individual within the team context, or with the whole group. Effective facilitation is about seeing what is required and finding ways that highlight or help resolve the issues at hand.

Teaching managers and front-line staff to facilitate is especially appropriate in the current working environment where empowerment is such a strong theme. Facilitation has a strong theoretical base and provides the necessary techniques to help managers move from command-and-control styles of management to the interdependent reality that is essential in modern organizations.

This does not suggest that a soft approach to facilitation is best. On the contrary, facilitation can be extremely tough. You might have to say things to people that they don't want to hear, or challenge unproductive or inappropriate behavior. It will certainly require from you the capacity to handle the full range of emotions—from delight to distress to anger to open appreciation. At the same time, you will need to be able to plan, to structure, to be creative, and to be authentic. This is what makes it such an exciting area of development. In this manual, we will explore all the key issues, helping you build up your skills as you become more self-aware. You can also use them directly with the teams and groups that you run.

Activity 1 Different Strokes for Different Folks

Facilitator Notes

There are differences between the roles of facilitator, trainer, and coach. Some of the qualities overlap, but as the table shows, there are differences in style and approach. Use this information as an introductory map from which to facilitate a general discussion, or give it to the participants to reflect on their own strengths and weaknesses in the areas indicated. (*Note*: This table is only a general representation of the main differences. Flexible professionals in any of these roles are likely to be able to serve in any of the three capacities.

	Facilitator or facilitative manager	*Trainer*	*Coach*
The core approach	Task and process-oriented focus. Agrees on a working contract with the group. Uses models, theory, insights, and activities to ensure understanding. Identifies process issues to achieve task or objectives. Establishes, maintains, and manages a valuing culture.	Content-focused delivery. Typically presentation-led, with activities used to reinforce message. The role of the trainer is to pass on knowledge or information.	Performance focused. Driven by the agenda of the coachee. Will focus on their goals and issues. The coach will clarify current situation and agree on actions with them.
The main intent	To serve the individual or team flexibly. To establish working contracts. To model effective behavior. To ensure effective working practices.	To lead the group. To carry learning agenda. To impart skill/knowledge.	To raise personal awareness of problems. To establish personal responsibility in tackling those problems.
Core qualities	Self-awareness. Empathy. Good intent. Confidence. Open-mindedness. Clarity. Discernment. Playfulness. Intuition. Flexibility.	Clarity. Structure. Confidence. Credibility. Knowledge.	Self-awareness. Perception. Interest. Attentiveness. Empathy. Confidence. Credibility. Structure.
Core skills	Listening. Speaking. Questioning. Culture setting. Challenging. Valuing. Observing. Containing.	Structuring. Presenting. Checking understanding.	Observing. Listening. Questioning. Challenging. Empathizing. Goal setting.
When to use	When you want full participation. When you want empowerment. When you want better teamwork. When you want new perspective. When you need change.	When you need to instruct. When you need to inform. When you need compliance.	When you want to support. When you want to empower. When you want to value. When you want to motivate.

Differentiators Between a Facilitator, a Trainer, and a Coach

Activity 2 Open Space

Facilitator Notes

The intention here is to highlight the importance of process as part of every task. Process involves the part of the iceberg that is under water (see model in theory section)—and we all have plenty of process we bring to every team or group! The question is, are we aware of our process and what happens to it in team scenarios?

1. Place a piece of flipchart paper in the center of the team/group.

2. Ask each participant to consider for a moment and to identify the following:
    a) a symbol for themselves in the team or group (for example, the participant might think that they are best represented by a star, a lightning flash, or a hand)
    b) a word for the contribution they can make in the team (for example, the word *insight*)
    c) the position they are taking/will take in the team or group (3 minutes)

3. Ask each participant to draw their symbol and write down their word on the blank piece of paper in any form they like. It is important that everyone contribute *within a 5-minute time limit.*

4. Once this is completed, ask the team or group to discuss the task. Here are some of the questions you might want to put up on a flipchart for them to reflect on:
    *   What did they notice during the task?
    *   Who did they notice during the task?
    *   How did they feel during the task?
    *   Did they either enjoy the task, dislike it, or feel neutral about it?
    *   What do they see on the paper?
    *   Would they like to change what they've done? Why? (10 minutes)

5. As facilitator, you will have observed the interaction of the team or group yourself. Offer and discuss feedback on your observations:
    *   Who started first? Who was last to contribute?
    *   Who took the central position? Who stayed on the sidelines?
    *   Who took the most space on the paper? The least?
    *   Who teamed up with others? Who stayed alone? (10 minutes)

How ready are people to share personal information? How willing and able do you feel they are to look at themselves as a team? You may want to drop some observations into the team discussion, such as "I was interested to see how long it took people to make their contributions; some of you were quite fast, others appeared happier to wait."

(continued)

Activity 2 Open Space (concluded)

This sort of intervention is neutral, but can bring a focus and depth to the discussions. See what happens to such an observation. Is it picked up? Don't worry if it goes nowhere; it might take some time for the team or group to consider their response. On the other hand, it might lead to immediate results and comment. Don't feel the need to explain. This type of intervention is called a process observation; let the team or group do with it what they will. Remain unattached to the outcome.

6. Finish the activity by taping the flipchart paper to the wall and acknowledging all input from the participants. Then ask them to keep in mind the contribution they want to make to the group process.

Coaching

As a coach, you can help raise awareness about the practical applications of facilitation skills for business situations. Consider with your coachee times and occasions when a facilitative approach might be appropriate (for example, if they are chairing a meeting or if they are in a consultative role with a client). It is important that they understand the context within which facilitation can be applied.

As coach, explain the theory around task and process, encourage the coachee to find out for themselves what facilitation is all about.

If there are specific issues on task and process that you believe the coachee needs to address, use questioning to draw out the coachee. Open questions and observations can help raise awareness and responsibility in the coachee. Beware of being too probing or too judgmental; this will simply lead to denial or defensiveness. The skill is in helping the coachee to consider the situation or concern in detail and examine how their behavior is or isn't helping the situation. What help do they need? How much control do they have over the situation? What is their bottom line? What are the options? What steps can they take? How will they know if what they have done has made a difference?

Facilitator Self-Development

There are three ways to find out more about facilitation.

1. Read about it. The key book is *The Complete Facilitator's Handbook* by John Heron. If this feels a bit heavy to start with, then you could also try *The Facilitation of Groups* by Hunter, Bailey, and Taylor. Alternatively, read the introductory sections in this manual. If you want to know more about coaching, start off with John Whitmore's very readable *Coaching for Performance*.

2. Watch it. Find qualified facilitators and observe them closely. Facilitators don't steal the limelight, but they do help others learn, express themselves, and come to decisions. Find someone whose style you like (and that seems to work), and model yourself after them.

(continued)

Facilitator Self-Development (*concluded*)

3. Experience it for yourself.

    a) Seek out situations where other people are facilitating a group you're in. Find yourself a coach, mentor, or counselor. Participate in workshops that are self-directed, and see if there are any opportunities to join action learning groups. If you want to go into the work in depth, consider group therapy so that you can explore group issues and see how group therapists help others with self-awareness and responsibility.

    b) Start to facilitate groups as a consultant, trainer, or manager. Be less directive, encourage contributions from other people, and listen to what *isn't* being said.

Finally, make facilitation part of your continuous professional development. Record what you do, what you read, and what you think. A major part of facilitation is self-awareness.

1.2 The Qualities of the Facilitator

Facilitation requires you to be as authentic as possible. It goes without saying that you can only help others in those areas that you first have explored and understood yourself. If you don't know how to deal with conflict yourself, then you should not expect others to work where there is disagreement or anger.

This means that you have to commit to your own personal development. You have to know what baggage you are carrying around, and be fully aware of your beliefs, feelings, experiences, hopes, fears, strengths, and weaknesses. It means facing up to who you are and who you are not, and knowing when and how you are likely to get triggered by others.

We have broken down the essential qualities that you are trying to develop as a facilitator into ten areas. Your challenge is to identify those areas in which you might need some development.

1. *Develop self-awareness.* This is the most important quality and needs constant attention. It is our self-awareness that enables us to be genuine. Perhaps it is impossible to ever know ourselves completely, but facilitators have to know their more-obvious flaws, hang-ups, and prejudices. You must be able to let your light shine through. (See Secton 1.7, Valuing Yourself and Others.)

2. *Be sensitive to others.* In teams and in one-to-one communication, facilitators need tremendous powers of perception and sensitivity. Effective facilitators are awake, moment by moment, in their minds, emotions, bodies, and spirit. They have great powers of concentration. They hold the boundaries of the group and they see what individuals or groups might need to help them move on.

3. *Be empathic.* At its most basic level, empathy requires us to understand the other person as if we were in their shoes—understanding their predicament. We must actively listen to them and reflect back, and not judge them.

4. *Have good intent.* The facilitator is there to serve others. This does not mean, however, that they need to be "nice." Sometimes the truth hurts, sometimes challenge is necessary, sometimes valuing somebody else is very difficult. An essential aspect of having good intent is to know why you are intervening and remain unattached to the outcome.

5. *Be confident.* This quality springs from competence. However, different people are confident in different ways. Some people are robust and self-assured. For others, confidence includes the ability to take risks and not be daunted by the unexpected. Confidence also implies a sense of trustworthiness. If you are trustworthy, people will be more likely to act on your suggestions and to move with you through change.

6. *Be open-minded.* Every meeting and every team is different and will present different challenges. You need to be resourceful and ready to adapt, but you don't need to have all the answers. You also need to be able to trust that others have the resources within them to find their own answers to the problems they are facing. They don't need you to do it for them.

7. *Be clear.* Clarity underpins the contracts a facilitator sets up with the team, as well as the boundaries that he or she establishes and the theoretical models that are presented. Clarity requires that you know what you are talking

about and that you know why you are working in the way you are. It is about imparting confidence to others and helping them make sense of the situation or problems with which people are faced.

8. *Be discerning.* Knowing when to intervene and how to intervene appropriately comes with experience. Have a light touch to start with, build up your skills little by little, be receptive to feedback, and watch and listen to others with as much attention as you can. When trying out new things, use inviting language ("Would you be willing to . . .?" or "I have a suggestion if you'd like to try looking at this from a different angle").

9. *Use humor.* It has been suggested that laughter is the shortest distance between two people. Facilitators who can find ways to introduce humor will find that it is a wonderful way to help people be less defensive and more open to change. However, have a light touch; we are not talking about joke telling here!

10. *Be intuitive.* Some people say that intuition comes from paying attention to the smallest details and picking up clues that to most people are invisible. Another way of looking at it is to be prepared to give credence to your inner wisdom. Listen to what you know inside yourself, stand by what you believe, and speak the truth. This doesn't mean that you always have to be right, but by listening to your intuition, you gain access to an extremely creative resource.

Activity 3 Physical Realities

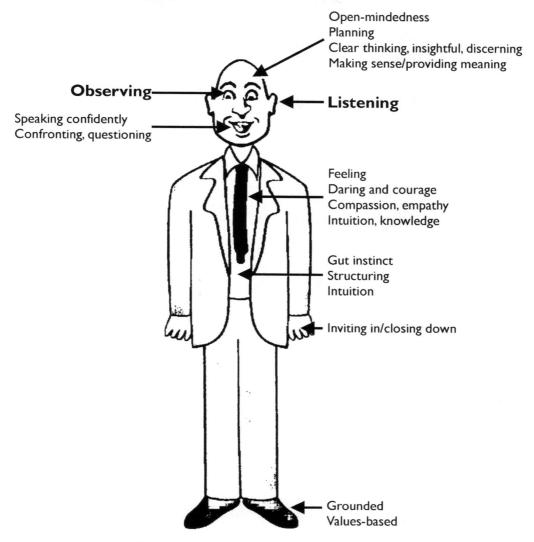

Open-mindedness
Planning
Clear thinking, insightful, discerning
Making sense/providing meaning

Observing

Listening

Speaking confidently
Confronting, questioning

Feeling
Daring and courage
Compassion, empathy
Intuition, knowledge

Gut instinct
Structuring
Intuition

Inviting in/closing down

Grounded
Values-based

Body Map: The Qualities of the Facilitator

Facilitator Notes

Facilitators should think of their own bodies as "tuning forks." We pick up signals from people at all sorts of levels, and we use our bodies to communicate in subtle and sometimes not-so-subtle ways. This activity encourages the team or group to map the qualities of facilitation onto the different areas of the body.

1. Provide the team or group with a body outline, or invite them to draw their own. Then, ask them to work in pairs or small groups to "map" as many of the qualities of the facilitator as possible onto the outline. Start by giving them an example such as mapping active listening onto the ears. (10 minutes)

2. Ask each group to present their findings to everyone. Place them onto one main body map or stick their sheets onto the wall as reminders of the qualities possessed by good facilitators. (5–10 minutes)

3. Have each small group consider what their strengths and weaknesses are in terms of the qualities that they've identified, and see if they can make a commitment to work together on those areas where they think they can improve. Suggest that members each get a buddy or coach to give them feedback at agreed-upon times regarding the quality or qualities they are trying to develop. (10 minutes)

Activity 4 Object Lessons

Facilitator Notes

This creative exercise is designed to encourage participants to see their uniqueness as facilitators and to gain feedback from others on how they are seen by others.

Materials: The facilitator will need a selection of objects and toys, such as shells and beach pebbles, children's toy models, small household objects, foreign coins, or odds and ends you might have sitting in a drawer.

1. Invite the participants to work in groups of three. Each member of the group will take a turn as *speaker*, *listener*, and *observer*.

2. Ask all the participants to select an object that they think best represents the qualities they have as a facilitator. If it is helpful, give the participants a theoretical example. For example, someone might choose a key because they see themselves as being able to unlock some doors but not others. The key can also be a symbol of authority, signify a way out, or represent something that allows them to shut things out. (5 minutes)

3. In their groups of three, ask the speaker to talk about the object he or she has chosen as a representation of the qualities he or she has. It is the task of the listener to listen actively, to paraphrase what the speaker has said, and to show that he or she has understood. If appropriate, the listener can ask facilitative questions to draw out the speaker about the qualities. It is the task of the observer to notice any dynamics between the speaker and the listener. (5 minutes)

4. After the five minutes have elapsed, the listener should be the first to give feedback on what it was like to facilitate. This self-assessment process should look at what the listener felt he or she did well and what, if anything, he or she would improve next time. The speaker should then give feedback on what it felt like to be facilitated, what the quality of attention was like, how empathetic he or she felt the listener was, and other qualities he or she displayed. The observer then adds his or her feedback. Was there anything missed or not said? (5 minutes)

5. Change the roles around so that the listener is now the speaker, the observer is the listener, and the speaker is now the observer. When this round is complete, change again so that everyone has had a turn as speaker, listener, and observer. (approx. 10 minutes per round)

6. Bring the groups back together and facilitate a discussion about the facilitating qualities they believe they possess and the qualities they observed in their small groups. What learning do they draw from this exercise? What skills might they need to develop? Have they made any connections between this brief exercise on facilitation and the interactions they have in their business lives? (10–15 minutes)

Coaching

There are a number of questions the coach should ask that might provide valuable insight about facilitation and help participants think about their approach:

- How can you offer your own insights about the process of facilitation?
- What are you most interested in learning about from others?
- If you are trying to help others develop themselves, what should you NOT do?
- Which quality are you most "attached" to?
- Which quality do you think will help you the most if you develop it?
- Which qualities do you think others see in you?
- Which of your qualities draws you to facilitation?

Facilitator Self-Development

There are a number of ways in which you can develop those qualities required for facilitation.

1. The next time you are in a crowded train or in a traffic jam, make a conscious note of your thoughts. Do you blame others? Do you judge others? Are you able to stay "in the moment," or are you thinking of all the things you have to do? See if you can find a place of stillness within yourself.

2. Write down a list of values you live by in both your personal life and work life. Be honest, and reflect on how closely you behave according to those values and how often you feel you don't adhere to them. What situations are most likely to make you compromise your values? What values do you expect other people to live by? Discuss this list with your coach.

3. With your partner, coach, or a trusted confidante, examine how well you nurture yourself. What do you expect of yourself? What comforts do you deny yourself? Who is there to look after you? Is this an easy or difficult piece of self-development?

4. Read as many of these helpful books as you can on this subject: *NLP at Work* by Sue Knight, *The Heart Aroused* by David Whyte, *The Empty Raincoat* by Charles Handy, *The Hungry Spirit* by Charles Handy, *The Soul at Work* by Roger Lewin and Birute Regine, and *The Complete Facilitator's Handbook* by John Heron.

1.3 Self-Awareness

Self-awareness is the most powerful and single most important quality that a facilitator can bring to a team or group. But what exactly is it?

One way of thinking about self-awareness is to see it as being open to yourself and understanding your own experiences, memories, thoughts, feelings, and sensations. Look at the way various people respond to each other: Someone with an aggressive attitude tends to force us to respond either by fighting back or backing off hurriedly almost without our thinking about it. This phenomenon, known as "behavior breeding behavior," can be changed. However, we need to be aware of our own triggers before we can pause and choose the best way to respond to such a person.

A person who is not self-aware does not realize the impact that they have on others. We see this all the time during conflict: people become entrenched in their own argument, refusing to see the value in the other person's argument. Conflict resolution starts with an awareness of how our own behavior affects the situation. Then we must accept some responsibility for the deadlock.

Self-awareness helps prevent us from falling into these sort of traps, but it also allows us to be more authentic and own up to our less-than-flattering behaviors, attitudes, and vulnerabilities. Paradoxically, it's by admitting our failings that we become more effective and accessible to others.

Self-awareness is directly connected with confidence and competence. When we are aware of what we do that works, we are more sure in our actions and our behavior. We know what our motivations are, and we are clear in our intent.

People with low self-awareness will not recognize their own competence and will often claim that any success they achieve is because of luck or being in the right place at the right time. Such modesty is actually self-defeating, because it denies people the opportunity to build their own self-esteem. It also limits their understanding of what skills they need to improve.

Awareness in Teams and Groups

There is no doubt that many teams and groups will be less effective if their facilitator has low self-awareness. If facilitators are uncomfortable with conflict, they are likely to want groups not to take risks. The group will always pick up on such dynamics and will consequently have little confidence in the facilitator's ability to handle disagreement. This behavior limits the group's ability to come up with new ideas and offer diverse perspectives.

Self-awareness enables us to tackle head-on those areas of discomfort that limit us. Being aware of emotions helps us discern how far we can go with others and what our personal limitations are. Let's say, for example, that there is a group member who irritates you. It is probably not all their fault: assume that this person is triggering something in you that is outside of your awareness. Perhaps they are mirroring your own behavior that you find hard to admit to, or they remind you of someone with whom you have unresolved conflict. Either way, it is useful to understand your own emotions and reactions, rather than become derailed. Self-awareness gives you the solid ground from which to take responsibility and appropriate action.

How to Develop Self-Awareness

It is worth saying that there is no one way to develop self-awareness. Whether you are a facilitator with a commitment to your own personal development or you are facilitating others to develop this quality, self-awareness is about opening doors, rather than determining a set route. Feedback is one common and effective way of building self-awareness, but even this simple technique is hard for many people. Other ways of building self-awareness are through reading, self-development exercises, learning groups, and coaching and mentoring experiences. Whatever approach you adopt, becoming more self-aware is challenging, but it is also rewarding, and worth the effort.

Activity 5 Empty Pockets

Facilitator Notes

This activity is about what participants carry around with them both literally and figuratively. You will need to start by presenting some theory on self-awareness and why it is important.

1. Ask participants to find a space for themselves in the room. Ask them to empty out either the bag they have brought with them or their pockets on their own and without talking to anyone. (5–10 minutes)

2. When they have had enough time to look closely at their possessions, ask them to partner up and talk about the items they carry with them, asking and answering the following questions:

    *   What do these objects represent?
    *   How do you identify with your objects?
    *   What characteristics are represented by the objects? Are any of these characteristics part of your personality?

    (15 minutes each)

Note: You might want instead to invite group members to bring in an object from home that has special significance to them, and ask the same questions. Alternatively, you could bring in a box of beads or odds and ends and ask each person to choose one that appeals to them. The same questions should be asked in each case.

Activity 6 Shoe Swapping

Facilitator Notes

This exercise is designed for a training group that needs to develop greater self-awareness and awareness of others. It will sound simple to some and complex to others. Write down the instructions or repeat them a few times until people get the hang of it. The objective is to help participants be more aware of the impact of their perceptions.

1. Ask participants to pair up and each take a couple of minutes to recall someone with whom they have had a recent disagreement or someone they aren't getting along with. (2 minutes)

2. Then ask each partner to take 5 to 10 minutes working through the following:

    *   Imagine yourself stepping into the shoes of the other person to see what life is like from their perspective. (You may want to adopt their posture, phrases, mannerisms.)
    *   Pretend you are this other person. Talk to your partner about their relationship with you: what they see in you, how they get along with you, and how they would like things to be with you. (At this stage, it is tempting for the speaker to lapse into responding from their own point of view, but it is important for the listener to keep them on track by reminding them to stay in role.)

(continued)

Activity 6 Shoe Swapping (*concluded*)

- At the end of the 5 minutes, the speaker should discuss with the listener anything they may have learned or new insights gleaned about this other person and what effect these new perspectives have had on you. (15–20 minutes)

3. Discuss any general insights with the group. (10 minutes)

Activity 7 Lifelines

Facilitator Notes

This activity helps people look at their past, their present, and their future, focusing on what has happened to them in life, the choices they have made, and the messages they carry around.

Materials: Sheets of flipchart paper and colored markers.

1. Ask participants to each draw a line on the paper that represents their life. At one end of the line, they should mark where they were born, and on the other end, when they expect to die. The line can be any shape and color. Ask people to indicate where they are now on that line.

2. Ask them to mark on the line they have drawn the most significant events that have happened in their lives: deaths, births, celebrations, rites of passage, major changes in health, and so on.

3. Ask them to answer the following questions about the events:
   - What made them significant?
   - Were they peak experiences or trough experiences?
   - What did they learn from them?
   - Which if any of these events did they choose to make happen? (10 minutes)

4. In pairs, ask people to talk about their lifelines:
   - Why did they draw the line the way they did?
   - Are there any surprises?
   - Do any patterns emerge?
   - What about the future? Where does the line go? (20 minutes)

   Remind people that there are no right or wrong answers here. The exercise is simply a way of helping them learn more about themselves.

5. Discuss any general insights with the team or group. Remind participants that the journey to self-awareness is a continuous one and is directly related to successful facilitation. (10–15 minutes)

Coaching

Increasing an individual's self-awareness means challenging the individual to think about where they are going and what they are doing with their lives. These are very deep, existential questions, but they will help participants examine those qualities that are so helpful in interpersonal relations (e.g., self-worth, authenticity, attentiveness, presence). Too many people separate their true selves from who they think they have to be at work. Help those you coach play to win by working with them to

- explore their values;
- explore their ambitions and talents;
- create a personal motto or statement that reflects who they are;
- have a vision and plan of the future they want; and
- help them through any obstacles they meet on the way.

Facilitator Self-Development

There are a number of ways in which you can raise your self-awareness.

1. Keep a journal or diary about your thoughts, dreams, hopes, feelings, memories, and daily experiences. Use drawings and inspirations, and don't be afraid to reveal your dark thoughts. Commit to the journal and look back on it every month to see what you have experienced and what you have learned.

2. Find out about the Johari Window.

3. Consult as many of these resources as you can: *Play to Win* by Larry Wilson and Hersch Wilson; *The Human Element* by Will Schutz; *NLP at Work* by Sue Knight; *The Seven Habits of Highly Effective People* by Stephen Covey; *Self-Development* by Dave Megginson and Mike Pedler; *The New Unblocked Manager* by Francis and Woodcock; and *Long Walk to Freedom* by Nelson Mandela.

4. Improve your emotional intelligence. If you are feeling uncomfortable in groups or detecting strong feelings that are unusual, ask yourself the following questions:
    - Is this my feeling? Am I uncomfortable, anxious, or tense?
    - Is this a feeling that belongs to someone else in the room that I am picking up from them?
    - Is this feeling part of the group dynamic (and thus needs to be addressed)?

    This awareness can help you make a decision about what to do next. If it is something you are detecting in the group, consider raising the issue; for example, say, "I am feeling quite tense. I wonder if that is how others in the group are feeling, and what that might mean for the group."

5. Notice what songs you sing or hum when you wake up in the morning or go about your day. What messages do you tell yourself that are embedded in the songs? (For example: "I took on a large project the other day, and I found myself singing 'Help' by The Beatles. I realized that I can't do the project all on my own, and that was why the song popped in to my head.")

1.4 Beginnings

Whether you are leading a new team, meeting a new client, establishing a learning group, or starting work as a new coach or mentor, you will need to pay attention to beginnings.

Many one-to-one and group meetings in business are, unfortunately, called with very little thought. Consequently, they often prove to be a waste of time. When you as a manager or facilitator want full participation—especially when you are going to be working with people over an extended period of time—you must think first about just what issues people might be grappling with at the time you get them all together.

For groups and teams, beginnings are an important part of what is known as the "form" stage of development. When people come together, they should know why they are there and have some idea of what to expect. During the forming process, the team becomes organized, roles will be clarified, goals are made clear, and the ways of working will be agreed upon or explained.

Facilitators can structure and try to enforce these requirements, but when people first come together, their own process issues will inevitably get in the way. If you have been to training events, you are probably familiar with some of the devices that trainers use to try to break the ice. Icebreakers are used because many people find it hard to contribute to groups when they don't know the people around them. They feel anxious, and this gets in the way of whatever it is that they are there to do or learn. In groups or teams where people know they will be spending time together, there will be a great deal of observing, posturing, and what is sometimes called "ritual sniffing." Whatever the team's or group's explicit task, the people involved will be focusing in the beginning on interpersonal dynamics. Some

people will set out to make an impression by talking about their experience, by asking questions, or even by being late. Others will do the opposite, finding ways to hide (they suddenly absorb themselves in reading or hiding behind their drink or newspaper).

The facilitator will also be affected by "beginning issues" and the associated anxiety they bring. The only difference between you and the group is that you have more control over the agenda.

When people are anxious, their behavior is more predictable. An easy way to see how this anxiety can manifest itself is by thinking of your first day at work in your current job. How did you prepare yourself? Did you find out as much as you could about the company? Or did you ignore the reality of the change until the last moment? What were your hopes and expectations about the team you'd be working with? How did you dress for that first day? Did you arrive early? Exactly on time? Or were you unconcerned about your punctuality?

We all have our own ways of coming into new groups and teams. As facilitators, we need to be aware of these anxieties so that we aren't tripped up by them at the start of our work. If people are anxious, their retention of information will be poor. The best thing is to talk about what we go through at the start of a new experience. This will allow people to be present mentally and emotionally as well as physically.

How to Work with Beginnings

You must signal that a change is about to happen. At the start of a meeting, acknowledge people's promptness or even do a quick check with them to see if there is any outside "clutter" that they need to deal with first.

If you are in a workshop or are working with a group that is going through major change, you may have to be more explicit about the significance of the experience and the feelings that are linked to them. For example, you might say, "This new project is specially convened because . . ." In so doing, you give participants a sense of the part they will play in the bigger picture.

You can acknowledge feelings simply by including a sentence about what you think might be going on (e.g., "I know some of you are curious about why we are here . . . I know feelings are running high for some of you, and I welcome all views in this meeting. Some of you might be anxious, so I will try to allay some of those concerns").

The key issue here is to acknowledge that you expect people to bring their personal agendas and baggage and give people a chance to settle. You'll find that you will get their full attention when you start with the work agenda.

Activity 8 Four-Way Meetings

Facilitator Notes

The goal of this activity is to give people the opportunity to share some basic and personal information when they first meet. It is usually a very popular exercise because participants get a better sense of one another when they can communicate who they are rather than just what they do.

1. Explain that this is an introductory exercise that breaks the ice at all levels. Each participant must introduce him- or herself at all levels: mind, body, emotions, and belief.

2. (Focusing on the *mind*) Ask the participants to find a partner and take three minutes to tell that partner about their background, their education, their job, and their interests. It is the partner's task to listen actively and try to get a real sense of who that person is and what keeps them occupied and interested on a day-to-day basis. (total of 6 minutes)

3. (Focusing on the *body*) With a different partner, each participant then speaks for three minutes about their physical health. What has their physical life been like in the past and up to today? Have they had major illnesses or accidents? Do they like sports and exercise? What do they do to keep themselves healthy? What is their diet like? Again, it is the partner's task to listen actively and to get a sense of who that person is and what their physical reality is like. (total of 6 minutes)

4. (Focusing on the *emotions*) With a different partner, participants take 3 minutes to speak about their emotional life (about their family and those relationships that mean most to them). What does friendship mean to the participant, and how do they keep such friendships going? The partner's role is to listen actively and to try to get a sense of the speaker's emotional life. (total of 6 minutes)

5. (Focusing on *beliefs*) Each person speaks for three minutes with a different partner about what it is that gives them a sense of meaning in life—things like world view, their creative expression, and their spiritual beliefs. It is the listener's task just to pay attention and to try to understand what is important to the speaker—not to engage in debate or judge the speaker. (total of 6 minutes)

6. When the exercise is over, allow people to reflect on and discuss the importance of beginnings. Talk about the importance of people needing to feel that they belong before they are able to contribute to the group. See if anyone on the team has any feedback about the exercise. Has it helped them feel more "present"? What parts of the activity did they find easiest? Which were most difficult? How easy was it for them to listen without their own thoughts intruding? (10–15 minutes)

Note: This exercise can be adapted to the size of the group and the time you have available. For example, if time is short or the group is large, have people change partners frequently.

It is not necessary for everyone to meet everybody else at every level. The point is for people to share something of themselves at different levels with different members of the team or group.

Activity 9 My Friend in the Chair

Facilitator Notes

This exercise asks participants to open up and talk about themselves. It encourages self-awareness. Take 5 minutes to explain the exercise and demonstrate how it works. Give people 5 minutes to reflect on how they feel and behave at the beginning of a workshop, etc., and write down a few words or phrases about these observations. Allow people to share for 2 to 3 minutes each.

1. Explain to the team or group that this activity requires them to talk about themselves as if they are their own best friend.

2. Demonstrate to the group how this works. Stand up behind your own chair and talk about yourself as though you are still sitting in the chair. For example. . .

> This is Anthony. When he first joins a group, Anthony is a little nervous. He often carries books or a newspaper around with him so that if he can't find anyone to talk to, he has something to do. He usually has a cup of tea or coffee in his hands, which is another useful prop. However, Anthony is really quite friendly and he enjoys meeting new people. If you speak to him, you'll see that he'll ask you lots of questions, because he's a good listener and he wants to find out who you are. That makes him feel safer. But remember to ask him questions, or else he'll feel disappointed.
>
> Anthony will get agitated if there's too much theory or the talking goes on for too long. He'll ask questions to keep himself awake, but he prefers to get involved in doing things and trying things out. He really enjoys project work. He brings energy to teams and believes that working together is usually far more effective and enjoyable than working alone.
>
> Anthony is married and has two young daughters. He is passionate about soccer and loves walking along a river. He has written a series of articles for his local newspaper about the history of his hometown.

3. If you want to keep this exercise moving, be directive and ask the person on your left to start. If you have a little more time and want to see what emerges, let people choose when they want to speak. See who goes first and who waits until the end, and facilitate a discussion about what people bring with them that they don't normally show, and how this affects working groups.

Activity 10 Ritual Beginnings

Facilitator Notes

This exercise focuses on the rituals that people tend to follow when they first start in a group.

1. Explain how many people observe superstitious rituals when they start a new venture (e.g., wearing lucky clothes, taking particular routes to work, being early or late, bringing a lucky charm). Tell a story about your own "beginning" rituals to illustrate what you mean. If you don't have any, use examples you've heard about, such as the athlete who always has to put his socks on last before going onto the field, or the woman who always wears black and white at the first meeting because she feels it gives her clarity. (5–10 minutes)

2. Have participants form small groups and swap stories of their own beginnings. What do they do? How do they behave? What idiosyncrasies do they have? (10 minutes)

3. Facilitate a discussion in the group and talk about the importance of recognizing and respecting beginning rituals.

Coaching

Individuals learn in different ways. Knowing and being able to recognize various learning styles helps the facilitator and team members better understand one another. This can be done in a team setting or on a one-to-one coaching basis.

For this exercise, you will need a learning styles questionnaire available through your training/personnel department. (Alternatively, consult the HRD Press online catalog at HRDpress.com.) What a learning styles questionnaire identifies is an individual's preferred learning style. Here are the four basic styles:

- *Activists* involve themselves fully in the here and now. They are open-minded and enthusiastic, and will be more than happy to give something a try. They enjoy business games, role-playing exercises, and new experiences. They do not like solitary work or being asked to review experiences. They are bored by implementation and long-term consolidation.

- *Reflectors* ponder experience. They collect data and ponder over it before coming to any conclusions. Their philosophy is "look before you leap." Within a learning group, reflectors provide information about the facts the group should be considering. They have a wide view and do not like being put in the limelight.

- *Theorists* like to see things as part of a system, model, or concept. They think problems through and like structure and clear purpose. They dislike what they perceive to be gimmicks and are not attracted to emotional experience. They want ideas and techniques to be well-founded and logical.

(continued)

Coaching (*concluded*)

- *Pragmatists* want to try things out to see if they work. They want to get on with things quickly and tend to be impatient with too much reflection and theory. They respond well to learning experiences that have a direct link back to their job, such as action learning.

You can use these styles to help the individual think about how they prefer to learn and how they deal with a team member who has a different learning style.

Facilitator Self-Development

1. Experiment with your learning styles. If you are basically an "activist" learner, see if there are ways that you can develop, say, a stronger theoretical understanding. Might it help you in your work? Look for ways to demonstrate what you know.

2. Read *The Facilitator's Fieldbook* by Tom Justice and David Jamieson, or *Transitions* by William Bridges.

3. Reflect on your own history. What do you do when you start something new? How do you make yourself feel safe or feel that you belong? Ask yourself these questions:

   - Do I have any rituals (special clothes, diets, etc.)?
   - How do I make my entrance? (Am I loud or soft? Do I hide, or try to engage?)
   - What role (leader, observer, team player, maverick, joker) do I take in new groups?
   - What needs to happen for me to take my place in the team or group?

4. Take a risk. If you are normally quiet, try to talk at the next new meeting you go to.

1.5 Planning and Structuring

Before walking into any kind of team situation or meeting, the facilitator must plan ahead. Too many groups go awry due to lack of forethought. A little time spent in preparation can prove invaluable.

You need to be clear about the purpose of the group or meeting, how long it will last, who the audience is going to be, and what their expectations are. Armed with this information, you can then decide on the most appropriate style of leadership and decide how to manage the time and plan for contingencies.

Before the planning stage, however, the facilitator must be fully appraised of the purpose of the meeting and why it is thought that a team or group solution is the best way to address the issue. It is useful to know beforehand if it is a meeting to exchange information or is a focus group, a problem-solving group, or one with a creative purpose. A feasibility study to discover whether or not the team or group has top-level support is also useful, as there may need to be negotiations about who attends (particularly if management staff, who control resources, are needed to answer questions).

Understanding Group Behavior

When you are about to facilitate any new group, remember that people will normally be anxious. They should be given information on start and finish times, break times, goals and objectives, and what is expected of them. The facilitator should provide guidance and advice about what to do and how to go about any tasks the group has been set early on.

As the group progresses, however, members will begin pushing the boundaries that have been established, and people will jostle for position in the group. Expect all kinds of behavior as group members try to influence each other and the facilitator. Some people may be resistant to tasks, some may get into conflict, some may try to control the group. As facilitator, you need to be prepared to deal with these behaviors and focus on your charter. (You will also need to remember that this behavior is a normal part of the group process.) Listen to contributions, reassert the objectives, and stay neutral. The group will eventually settle into a more productive and cooperative way of working, and a group culture will emerge with its own written and unwritten norms.

Structuring

Much of what happens in groups cannot be planned. This can be alarming for facilitators who want to know exactly what is coming, so keep in mind that facilitation requires flexibility. Learn how to structure "in the moment."

Every meeting is a unique blend of personalities, moods, external pressures, and organizational goals. Facilitators must be able to adapt to the immediate needs, and to trust their experience, knowledge, and even gut instinct. Interventions you might need to make might include raising the awareness of the group to what is going on, changing the energy, introducing an appropriate activity, coaching someone on a new skill, or even challenging behavior. You must be sensitive, aware, and watchful of the behavior and feelings of individuals and the whole group.

When I use the term *structuring*, I mean being able to provide what is needed at that moment. I once ran a teamwork event where one of the team suddenly declared on the second day that he was simply no longer prepared to work with his female manager, who was in the room. He demanded to know what I was going to do about it.

I was shocked, and so was the team. It is in situations like this that you need to have some "structures" to fall back on. The manager was unable to address the situation in the team then and there and agreed to work with both individuals outside the team context and do some conflict resolution. The structure I used involved the two parties listening to each other and then trying to see things from each other's point of view. The details aren't important—what is important is to realize that facilitators need to have techniques to fall back on. Then they can even enjoy the unexpected.

Activity 11 Group-Planning Checklist

Facilitator Notes

Use this checklist as a planning guide for groups. Not all the items will be relevant to every group or meeting that you run, but it can serve as a prompt for planning the early stages. Sound planning at this stage provides every group with a solid base and helps you avoid pitfalls.

- *Purpose:* Identify the need for the meeting/group, and make sure you have clear goals and objectives. If any key people need to be there, make sure they are invited.

- *Communication:* Make sure that integral people are clear about the intention of the meeting/group and give them appropriate background information.

- *Contracting:* Share the goals and objectives with the group at the outset so that everybody is clear about the agenda.

- *Confidentiality:* Agree on what happens to the results of the meeting and who the feedback should go to. You may need to work out a contract regarding confidentiality.

- *Contingency:* Think how you would deal with the very thing you hope you never come across as a facilitator. What will you do when your nightmare scenario begins to present itself in your group? Have a contingency plan.

- *Diversity:* Think about how you will handle diversity issues in the meeting or group. Be sure you are unbiased and are fair to all represented there.

- *Structuring:* Plan how you will address different styles of learning within the group. Some groups or meetings will be more discussion-based, while others will call for a variety of techniques and skills so that you get the most out of the group.

- *Leadership style:* What style of leadership is most appropriate for this group or meeting? Do you need to be authoritarian? Cooperative? Or encouraging of group autonomy?

- *Practicalities:*
  —Is the room booked?
  —Who has to be contacted in an emergency?
  —Do other users of the building need to know that about the program?
  —Is a greeter necessary?
  —Where is the fire exit?
  —Are all the materials and facilities you might need available?

Activity 12 Worst-Case Scenario

Facilitator Notes

To prepare fully for any group or meeting, the facilitator needs to prepare for a nightmare scenario. Nightmare scenarios are different for everyone; think about what yours might be and how you should deal with it if and when it occurs.

1. Ask people to reflect on the following questions:
    *   Think of a group or team with whom you are about to work, and imagine what could possibly go wrong. What absolute nightmare scenario would you want to avoid at all cost?
    *   Who would that situation involve, and how would it manifest itself?
    *   What kind of behavior would it require from participants and from you? What would the other people present be doing?
    *   How do you envision yourself dealing with it?
    *   How would you like to deal with it (ideally) in order for it not to be a disaster?
    *   Imagine watching the scenario through a camera lens. Be objective about what you see, and describe what each person is doing. Highlight what is useful and what is not helpful. Looking through this lens of objectivity, describe what could be done instead. Pretend you are an independent third party watching the action. This may give you some insights into how to manage the situation if and when it occurs. (15–20 minutes)

2. Ask people to pair up and describe to each other what their worst-case scenario is and how they would deal with it. See if their partner has any helpful suggestions. (5–10 minutes each)

3. Share any insights with the whole group. If you can, provide some real examples where contingency planning was essential. (10–15 minutes)

Activity 13 Collaboration Checklist

Facilitator Notes

From time to time, you may be asked to work with other people in a training or managerial capacity. If that is the case, plan in advance how you will work together. There will be inevitable differences in what you know and the approach you take, so be clear about the following:

- Who will do what (introductions, ground rules, agenda setting, leading the discussion, and so on).

- Who will organize the resources in the room (OHP, room booking, and so on).

- What role each person will play to make a clear contribution to the running of the event. (If one person dominates, the other might end up feeling like the magician's assistant with nothing much to do.)

- How you will deal with conflict between yourselves, and what you will do if participants get into conflict.

- What you expect from the group. For example, if the meeting is about finding out people's views on something, then discuss your own views of the situation beforehand. This will help you know where you are both coming from when you are in front of the group. If you have differing views and values, make sure you know what these are and how much you are willing to share with the group.

- How you can support each other. (There will be behavior that one of you finds easier to deal with than the other; agree on who will deal with what.)

- How you will manage any good cop, bad cop attitudes.

- Perceived weaknesses and perceived strengths as facilitators. Discuss this together so that you can be flexible and supportive of each other.

- Ways of not becoming competitive with each other in front of the group. Consider clearly negotiating goals and roles in advance.

Coaching

In your one-to-one work with staff members, find out how they prepare for important events such as job interviews, speeches, holidays. Help them recognize their patterns of behavior and their usual methods and approaches. Do they over-prepare? Do they under-prepare? Are they theoretical in their approach, or instinctive? Explore with them the gaps in their planning, as well as those aspects that they are good at.

If you are coaching someone who lacks confidence, emphasize the need for contingency planning. What will happen if things go wrong? Do they have any fall-back plans? What can they rely on if their first approach doesn't work?

Finally, it may be helpful to work with your coachee on learning styles to establish which is their preferred style. A self-assessment can be used as a coaching tool to help people see for themselves what approach to learning they might naturally take and what they might normally leave out.

Facilitator Self-Development

1. The best preparation for a group or meeting is preparation that is suited to your learning style. A reflector might go for long walks and imagine what might happen and how it will be dealt with. An activist might not bother to prepare, but will be willing to enjoy being put on the spot and learning from the experience. A theorist is likely to read everything they can on any topic that might come up about the company, plus several facilitation books (just in case). The pragmatist will probably read relevant articles and give some thought to the event, but will really prefer to get on with it and see what happens.

2. Whatever your style, stay grounded. Find a way of connecting to yourself, and remind yourself of how good a facilitator you are. Try this by keeping your feet firmly on the ground. Breathe deeply so that oxygen can circulate and energize your whole system. It is amazing how many people forget to breathe properly when they are anxious, and rush their words. Their voice becomes thin and breathless, and they look as nervous as they are.

3. Remember that you are competent. Be fully aware of your own talents, skills, and resources. Review them, make a list, and add to them regularly through further training and development. This helps you to stay consciously competent and to identify any gaps in your knowledge. Bluffing is not a good substitute for knowing what you know and feeling secure in that knowledge.

4. Practice self-talk. Develop positive self-talk and repeat it regularly, especially when you find yourself engaging in negative thinking. If you are interested in neurolinguistic programming, learn about "anchoring," where you consciously find words, images, or gestures from non-related activities that recall the experience, state, or attitude you want.

5. Don't be afraid of superstition. Many people are superstitious, taking particular routes to work, wearing lucky clothes, or going through careful routines that worked for them the last time. Use such rituals consciously and lightly if they help you feel good about yourself.

1.6 Drawing Up a Group Contract

Drawing up a working contract with a team or group is a vital aspect of facilitation. However, there are two different aspects of contracting that you will need to address.

1. *Primary contracting* involves explaining the purpose of any meeting and reminding participants about

   • goals and objectives;
   • practical arrangements such as health and safety (e.g., location of the fire escape, break times, duration of sessions, venue information);
   • expectations of participants (what they are there to learn or do); and
   • expectations of you as leader/facilitator (who you will be reporting back to, your role, etc.).

In primary contracting, you establish and demonstrate the style and authority of the manager or facilitator. As the leader of a team or group, you will need to make a decision as to how much power you will exert and how much you will give to others.

In this respect, you have three power bases to operate from: *authoritarian*, *cooperative*, and *autonomous*. The level of authority you choose to exert will impact directly on the amount of negotiation the group will have over the contract.

In an *authoritarian* approach, the leader will make all the major decisions about the group or team and the contract. Members will then decide whether or not to accept what is essentially a predetermined package. This might be appropriate, for example, in situations where expert information is being imparted; participants are there to be informed. They might be able to ask questions, but contributions and interventions are not expected.

In a *cooperative* approach, both sides (the group or team leader and members) draw up the contract. The leader can introduce some broad aims and objectives, but the parameters will stretch or squeeze according to the needs of the group. The contracting will be negotiated between group members and the leader within these defined parameters. (This happens in training, for example, when people attending skills-based courses are asked to influence the content of the training according to what skills they need to learn).

In *group-autonomy*, the group or team leader will only help the team form and meet. Members will take responsibility for their own goals, decisions, and ways of working. Contracting issues are agreed upon by members, rather than by the group and the facilitator (for example, when the aim of the facilitator is to empower all participants).

Facilitators will typically have to use all three styles from time to time in the team or group. The challenge for all facilitators is to be aware of their own preference and make sure that the mode they are using is appropriate to the needs of the team or group.

2. *Secondary contracting* is just as important as primary contracting. It addresses the emotional and often unspoken needs of the team or group, and focuses on the conditions necessary to raise participation levels. (This is often done in the

form of ground rules.) The way this contracting is handled will greatly impact team or group culture.

In secondary contracting, facilitator authority is also extremely relevant. The facilitator can impose a list of ground rules (authority), work out with the group what the ground rules are going to be (cooperative) or leave the decision and process of making ground rules to the team or group (autonomy).

It is worth noting, however, that misunderstandings can arise when authority is misused or there is lack of clarity about how decisions are made. An organization about to embark on restructuring once invited staff members to a consultative meeting. Everyone had their own ideas on what the best form of restructuring would be and they were ready to give their opinions, but were told what was going to happen, by when, and how many redundancies would take place. They were dismayed and angry at the authoritarian nature of its delivery. There was no consultation at all. If the company had said it was going to make an announcement, staff would not have been happy, but they would have been more accepting of how it was done. Facilitators who make the mistake of appearing cooperative but are then dictatorian will often end up in such stormy waters, wondering where it all went wrong.

Activity 14 A Model for Group Work

This activity helps the group reflect on the process of secondary contracting and determine what it needs from others. Done successfully, it will help the group form its own identity and culture, which is necessary for effective group functioning. It is best used at the very beginning of group work, after the introductions and primary contracting have taken place.

Facilitator Notes

The goal is to involve group members in creating the conditions necessary for them to work together in an atmosphere of safety and challenge. This model can help a group establish a list of ground rules. The activity often enables people to discuss their needs (which might make the explicit drawing up of a list of ground rules unnecessary).

1. Draw the model below on a flipchart and explain each step to group members. (10 minutes)

Adapted from the Professional Development Group

- *Safety.* Group work begins here. We all have "safety" needs, and never more so than when in a group. Therefore it is important to reflect on what things make it safe enough for you to take risks in a group. (For example, do you need to know that what is said will not be repeated elsewhere? Do you want to be treated in a certain way?)
- *Openness/Honesty.* Once we feel safe, we can be more open and authentic. This provides an opportunity to explore concerns and to be more creative as a group. It sounds simple, but what do you need as an individual to bring more of your self, your views, and your uniqueness into this room?
- *Trust.* Openness and honesty breed trust. It is important to trust others and to be treated as someone who is trustworthy. How will you know when trust is high in this group? What will you or others be doing? And what will make trust levels plummet for you and others?
- *Challenge.* Once trust has been established, people can start to challenge and be challenged, and accept that this feedback is genuine. Challenge is the gateway to change and development if it is delivered with good intention, clarity, and honesty. Punitive criticism or dealing with unfinished business under the guise of challenge is not acceptable. A person or a group can only rise to a challenge if the challenger has earned respect and is perceived to have no personal axe to grind. What do individuals or the group need to do to foster challenge as part of a healthy, constructive climate in the group?
- *Change/Development.* Once the previous four conditions are met, change and development will occur in individuals and the group or team.

(continued)

Activity 14 A Model for Group Work (*concluded*)

Note: Although this model looks linear, it is not. People will place themselves at different starting levels, depending on their relationship with the group and each other. Levels will also fluctuate according to what is happening within the group. For example, trust levels may dip if someone joins the group who isn't well known. "Safety" can be a problem for some if an argument breaks out in the group or if there are rumors of layoffs. So there is a contextual consideration of how far external forces impinge on the group. The important thing is for the group or individuals to recognize the stage they are in at any given time. This will raise awareness of what needs may have to be attended to.

2. Invite group members to pair up and discuss where they see themselves now on the model and what they want from the group now. (5 minutes)

3. Give each participant a piece of paper and ask them to write on it the stage they feel they are in at this moment in time. Translate the results onto the model with stars or dots to get a visual display of where the group sees itself. (5 minutes)

4. Ask people to feed back some of the flavor of their discussion so that you know what individuals need. This may result in requests for confidentiality (safety), plain talking (challenge), respect (trust), and so on. The discussion, if it is along these lines, is a sign that the group is creating its own culture and sharing expectations of standards of behavior. The group will have established a working contract from their own needs and wants, and will be far more likely to take responsibility for maintaining the contract than anything imposed by the leader. (10 minutes)

Note: There is a natural tendency to pay lip service to ground rules and render them meaningless by ritualizing them, not believing in them, being dubious about enforcing them, or not dealing with the cynicism surrounding them. It may be that you have participated in a group where ground rules were established and not adhered to. This model offers a way of getting the group to "walk their talk." It gives everyone in the room a legitimate right to question behavior that falls outside the established culture. Use the model every now and again to check out where group members are with it. Let it become a working tool that keeps group energy high and the process positive.

Activity 15 Con Tricks

Facilitator Notes

This is a light-hearted exercise designed to make contracting with the group more realistic (and to get their buy-in).

1. Pass out copies of the cartoon below to participants. Ask participants to work in twos or threes to discuss the various positions of the cartoon characters and their thoughts, feelings, and reactions. Ask them to bring back to the group the cartoon character that they most identify with and put their comments in a bubble on the cartoon.

   Ask them also to think about how they can take some responsibility for the group contract (since it is meant to be something that is shared by the group, rather than imposed by the facilitator). This is particularly important in groups where sensitive issues may be discussed or where people feel threatened in some way (perhaps by organizational changes). (10–15 minutes)

2. Facilitate feedback and a discussion based on the cartoon reflections. This discussion is designed to overcome some of the resistance group members have been feeling about contracting, because you will give permission for the group to say the unsayable. Explain that contracting only works if there is a mutuality to it—that is, if all parties agree to it and see the benefit of it. (10–15 minutes)

3. Once this exercise is completed, the group should be in a position to create a clear contract about how they are going to work together. (A set of ground rules and a discussion can foster a climate of trust, openness, and understanding.)

Coaching

Establishing a contract for a one-to-one relationship has to be approached with confidence and sensitivity. It is important to negotiate the contract and to understand that both parties will benefit from the exchange. You as the coach might be building your coaching expertise, and the coachee might be drawing on the resources you have available. Don't make the mistake of thinking that the learning will only be one way: you, too, will be challenged and helped by the coaching. In establishing the contract, it is important to attend to three aspects:

1. *Practicalities*—Time of meetings; frequency; payment (if any); venue.

2. *Professionalism*—Awareness of the expectations of each other; exploring objectives for the session; verbally stating the contract for each session; exploring what might sabotage the success of the agreed-upon goals, exploring how successful outcomes will be measured.

3. *Process*—Building trust and rapport in the relationship; raising awareness of any third-party interest in the contract (such as line manager or HR); periodically checking for hidden agendas; exploring any resistance.

This may seem a lot to take in to account when beginning to coach somebody. However, once it becomes part of your natural style as a coach, the contracting process will provide a firm bedrock for building effective relationships and achieving clear, measurable results with coachees.

Facilitator Self-Development

1. Read *TA for Trainers* by Julie Hay (McGraw-Hill, 1992).

2. Attend a basic coaching course (some of the interventions in coaching are great for use in groups).

3. Try negotiating a clear contract with children, and keep them to the contract.

4. Observe and model people who make clear contracts in meetings.

1.7 Valuing Yourself and Others

Valuing is a key dimension in facilitation. It refers to your ability to create a climate of respect for people and their personal autonomy.

In effect, we are talking here about the integrity of facilitation—the ability of facilitators to build trust and to create a supportive climate that honors and respects the individual or team they are working with. The aim of valuing is to build a climate in which people can be genuine—a climate in which they feel free and willing to disclose their reality, which keeps them in touch with their true needs and interests.

As we have seen with other aspects of facilitation, you have a choice of styles.

1. *Authoritarian.* The facilitator who works out of this mode can achieve much by setting clear ground rules and by expressing positive feelings to people in the team. Such expression has to be authentic, of course, and the facilitator has to be in touch with his or her own genuine thoughts and feelings.

    Some examples of the facilitator working in this mode might be

    - standing up for the values that have been agreed to in the contract (honesty, risk taking, vulnerability, confidentiality, etc.);

    - reaching out to people and expressing care and concern when another person is experiencing distress (and in so doing demonstrating their values to you); and

    - positively affirming the qualities in another person and highlighting aspects of their being or behavior that they or the team might be undervaluing.

2. *Cooperation.* The whole issue of valuing implies sharing responsibility with others. By working cooperatively, the facilitator will be building trust and valuing people. One of the key words for the facilitator here is *choice*. Working in this mode, the facilitator will honor the choice that others make and prompt others to adopt a nurturing, validating, and supportive behavior. This will help build and establish a valuing climate.

3. *Group autonomy.* It may well be the facilitator's goal to get the group to be autonomous. This doesn't mean letting go completely of the individual or team; rather, it implies that you have established a culture that is innately more self-directed and mature. In this situation, people naturally value each other. It is your role in this mode to be fully present with the individual or team, witnessing their emergence and interaction.

Self-Valuing

If this all sounds a bit too easy, then it is worth remembering that many of us are far more familiar with criticism than praise.

The hardest work in facilitation is the preparation, and that means working on our own competence and confidence. If you doubt that this is so, then think of those parents who say how much they love their children and value them above anything else. Then consider how those same parents limit, undermine, and ignore the rights and needs of their children.

The point here is not about bad parenting; rather, it is about how hard it is to value someone else when we don't value ourselves. For example, if we've been taught when we were children that it is not acceptable to be mischievous and inquiring or the only praise we ever got was for getting the spelling test right or for keeping our rooms tidy, maybe we've ignored the parts of ourselves that are more spontaneous and creative. When we then face someone who expresses those qualities with some abandon, we find ourselves becoming unduly critical.

We need to do some self-reflection. Facilitators are not typically attracted to this role, because they want to take center stage. Those who are drawn to facilitation generally want to empower others. In the valuing dimension, this means that we need to know just how lovable we are and to know that it's all right to have a high opinion about ourselves.

Activity 16 I notice, I imagine, I feel

Facilitator Notes

This activity can be used in a number of ways. It is designed to help training managers and facilitators pay detailed attention to another person to help them become aware of the signals they pick up subconsciously that they might be able to use.

This activity is also an intervention in its own right. The timing is essential here, but it can, for example, be used with a team or group where trust is an issue or where you are looking for a structure to help highlight issues of diversity.

1. Ask participants to pair up. Explain that the objective is for them to sit or stand opposite their partner and make three statements (I notice, I imagine, I feel) to each other, based on their observations. A partner might go first and say, "I notice the lines around your eyes. I imagine you've been working hard recently, and I feel concerned about your health." (3–4 minutes per pair)

   Encourage people to take their time, check that their feelings are really feelings, and be sure that what they've imagined is true for the other person.

2. After both partners have swapped observations, they then find another partner until everyone in the team or group has been observed and has made observations about everyone else. (3–4 minutes per pair)

3. Facilitate a group discussion on what people experienced and observed: whether their observations were accurate; how it made them feel to be observed with such attention; what it made them feel about other people; whether there were any common themes that came up; and what blocks (if any) they experienced. (10–15 minutes)

Activity 17 Self-Disclosure

Facilitator Notes

This activity helps build trust within the team or group, and helps establish that appreciation, recognition, and valuing of others is not only important within the team, but is essential if you want to empower others.

1. Ask participants to think of one of the following situations:
   a) a mistake they have made at work that they feel uncomfortable talking about (this could be a mistake from the past or one made recently)
   b) something they value from their personal life that impacts on their work life but that they find difficult to talk about (5 minutes)

(continued)

Activity 17 Self-Disclosure *(concluded)*

2. Ask participants to pair up and take 15 minutes each to talk about the situation. It is their partner's task to facilitate the discussion and to demonstrate this valuing dimension by:

   - affirming the person and their experience;
   - appreciating and valuing the person's qualities;
   - being genuine;
   - respecting the rights and feelings of the person;
   - celebrating with that person, if appropriate, how they are dealing with the issue;
   - giving them their complete attention—being intense, alert, and supportive—and paying silent attention to the other.

3. Bring the discussion back to the large group and ask for feedback. Try to draw out the cultural issues that prevent valuing within the organizational culture. Highlight unhelpful feelings (anxieties, for example) and attitudes. Consider what might need to happen to change the situation. (10–15 minutes)

Activity 18 What car?

Facilitator Notes

This is an activity that highlights issues of trust and self-worth. Facilitators will need a light touch with this activity, because it can provoke hilarity and highlight people's inner worlds. It is appropriate for any work on personal development or for a group of facilitators-in-training who want to explore with others what issues they have about their own self-worth.

1. Ask people to think about what type of car they closely relate to. *Note:* This is not about what sort of car they want to buy, but rather how they would describe themselves in the busy traffic of business life. Ask them not to censor their thought processes, but rather to take the first model that comes up as being the one to work with. Ask them to write down the make and model on a piece of paper. (3 minutes)

2. Then ask them to think about what condition this car is in. Again, ask people to use their imagination. Ask them to think about the inside as well as the outside of the car, and to say what sort of care and attention they typically get from their owner, as well as what they actually need. Ask them to think about who uses "them" and how they are driven. Again, ask people to write it down. (5 minutes)

3. Ask the team or group to then get into pairs. Each member of the pair should pass their sheet to their partner. The partner reads the description and associated thoughts, and gives their view of what that car is worth, how reliable it is, where they see it as being most suitable (for example, city streets, country roads, or highways), whether it needs a tune-up or inspection, and how long it will continue to run. (10 minutes)

(continued)

Activity 18 What car? *(concluded)*

4. Once partners have given their feedback, participant A reflects back on what he or she has heard and if it's an accurate assessment of their car (or not). At this point, the partner should facilitate the discussion. Encourage them to talk about their car, the care they asked for, and the care they usually give themselves. What were they surprised by? What feelings came up? (10 minutes)

5. Once this stage is completed, ask the participants to shake off whatever feelings they expressed and have the partners switch roles. Repeat the process above.

6. Bring the group or team back together and consider the findings and experiences that people have had in relation to self-esteem and self-worth. The underlying question to consider here is this: How can we value others if we don't value ourselves? (10–15 minutes)

Coaching

Self-esteem is especially important in relationships, so if you are coaching someone on the subject, you need to model how to "value" people. If you haven't already done so, take a risk and affirm who the individual is. Find qualities that you admire. Find ways to reach out and show your concern.

Ask the coachee to consider what it means to value others and why it is important. Reflect with them on the relationships they have at work with colleagues, clients, suppliers. Which of these relationships do they most value? Why? If your coachee does not seem to see other people's value, then it might be important for them to look at their own self-esteem. Much will depend here on the experience of the facilitator and the appropriateness of asking someone to look at issues that might, more properly, belong to the world of counseling and therapy. The coach can legitimately ask the coachee to look at areas in which they are proud of themselves and draw out the connections between valuing ourselves and valuing others.

Facilitator Self-Development

The following suggestions can help you explore valuing:

1. Contemplate the following passage from Nelson Mandela's inaugural speech of 1994:

> Our deepest fear is not that we are inadequate.
> Our deepest fear is that we are powerful beyond measure.
> It is our light, not our darkness, that most frightens us.
> We ask ourselves, *Who am I to be brilliant, gorgeous, talented, fabulous?*
> Actually, who are you not to be?
> You are a child of God.
> Your playing small doesn't serve the world.
> There's nothing enlightened about shrinking
> so that other people won't feel insecure around you.

(continued)

Facilitator Self-Development (concluded)

> We were born to make manifest the glory of God that is within us.
> It's not just in some of us; it's in everyone.
> And as we let our own light shine, we unconsciously
> give other people permission to do the same.
> As we are liberated from our own fear,
> our presence automatically liberates others.

2. Read *The Complete Facilitator's Handbook* by John Heron; "The Art of Facilitation" by Young and Landale in *The Gower Handbook of Training and Development* (1999), *The Tibetan Book of Living and Dying* by Sogyal Rimpoche; and *Care of the Soul* by Thomas Moore.

3. Notice what people do for you. Find new words to appreciate them, and be sure to make eye contact.

4. If you have let a small dispute injure a great friendship, see if you can repair the damage.

5. Write your own obituary in the words of someone who loves you unconditionally. Express what qualities were most admirable and what achievements were most memorable. Write about your laughter and pain, about your playfulness and commitment. Write about what you have loved and about how different people you've known would remember you.

1.8 Managing Feelings

Feelings are often considered problematic in the workplace. The unspoken message we pick up from some organizational cultures is that strong emotions are embarrassing, so we must not express them.

However, feelings are an extremely important barometer. It is essential that facilitators who want to work effectively with others must be confident and competent when it comes to emotions.

Many of us are used to censoring our feelings, but we know that they are, nevertheless, always present. Put a group of people together, tune in to the group's mood, and you will quickly notice people feeling bored, irritated, amused, sad, angry, jocular, frustrated, and so on at different times throughout the meeting.

Must you manage all these feelings? Certainly not, but there will be times when you will have to address feelings directly. If you are a manager, your attitude and sensitivity to feelings will influence the work climate.

Of course, many people want to keep their emotions private, even when they are clearly being affected by them. They will resent it if you try to interfere. (This is fair enough.) In such cases, it is best to address the behavior that always accompanies emotion, rather than try to manage the feelings directly.

At the other end of the scale is the person who always appears to live in a state of heightened emotion. Their life is a drama in which they play out the roles of victim, rescuer, and persecutor. Such people will need careful handling because they will try to draw you into their world. They typically find it difficult to change, regardless of the time and attention you give them.

To manage this range of emotions, you must start by managing your own. What are your triggers? Which emotions do you enjoy, and which do you find distinctly uncomfortable? If you find it hard to express your own feelings, then you probably won't know what to do when others start to express theirs. It is also worth remembering that research on emotional intelligence suggests that your ability to manage your own emotions and understand what others are feeling is directly related to your effectiveness at work.

Unfortunately feelings also come with a lot of baggage. In British culture, for example, most men carry messages about being brave, not crying, and not showing vulnerability. Such messages can get in the way for facilitators, which is why it is so important, if you are working with others, that you make it a priority to explore and understand your own emotional baggage.

If you are building on this personal competence, here are some guidelines that can help in groups or teams:

- Accept that feelings are OK and that they give you a lot of information about the situations you are in.

- Develop curiosity about your own feelings. Observe them with affection and learn how to discriminate between them.

- Encourage discussion about feelings. Explore their impact and effect. Usually if one person in a group is feeling something strongly, others in the group will be feeling something similar.

- Remember that feelings shared in a group can remove barriers, lift energy, and help the group be more focused.

- Make sure, however, that attention to feelings does not take priority over the task—there has to be a balance between allowing time for process and focusing on the task.

- Explore with the group some of the beliefs and group norms that have emerged regarding emotional expression.

It is also important to appreciate what feelings are appropriate for the work setting. For example, you will have to make the distinction between emotional issues that are caused by something that has happened "here and now" in the group and those that are regressive hurt feelings from the past that have been restimulated in the present. For instance, if someone is particularly sensitive, it is useful to know whether it has to do with the topic of discussion or the fact that they have been reminded of some unfair treatment they experienced previously. This information can only be gleaned by inquiry, and the facilitator needs to feel confident both in addressing it and in his or her ability to handle whatever response he or she can get. This is emotional intelligence in action.

Activity 19 Speechless

Facilitator Notes

This activity helps people explore what it might be like to bring more of themselves into potentially charged situations. It also helps people see how much censoring they do of their own behavior and speech and what they think about the management of feelings in the workplace.

1. Provide participants with several sheets of paper and a pen.

2. Invite participants or team members to take 2 or 3 minutes to consider one situation in which they were involved where the management of emotions was an issue. If people can't think of a personal situation, a situation they have observed or even one from a film can be used instead. (3–4 minutes)

3. Ask each participant to write the following:
   - a "headline" about what they learned from this situation
   - one short paragraph about their strategy in the situation (what they actually did) (5 minutes)

4. Now ask participants to take a new sheet and divide it into two columns, and use the left-hand column to write a description of what happened. This should be written in the present tense and should take no more than two sides of the paper. (15 minutes)

5. In the right-hand column, ask participants to write what they didn't say but thought or felt at the time (and didn't reveal). (15 minutes)

6. In small groups of 3 or 4, ask participants to share their case studies (20 minutes each). Those listening should ask questions that will help the speaker explore what their feelings were and what stopped them from sharing them at the time. Additionally, the small group can consider how different the situation might have been if those thoughts and feelings had been shared.

Note: Look for opportunities to focus in on the emotions participants find difficult to share. It can sometimes be useful for two members of the group to role-play a scenario for this. The person whose issue it is can observe and then indicate what emotions they found especially difficult to deal with.

Activity 20 Like the Plague

Facilitator Notes

We all face situations that we don't like or would rather avoid. This activity helps us share our feelings about such situations. The intent here is to help a group or team recognize that such feelings are normal and that sharing them helps us confront them. However, it also highlights the strengths and weaknesses colleagues don't always share from which we can learn.

1. Ask participants to consider two or three work situations that make them feel uncomfortable. Examples include saying no to your manager, asking for help or guidance, and working on a team where nobody knows what to say or do. (5–10 minutes)

2. Now ask people to form small groups and share their dislikes. They should write these on a piece of flipchart paper so that the whole team or group can see what situations individuals might avoid. (15 minutes)

3. Facilitate a whole-group discussion (20–30 minutes) about these difficult situations, and try to get participants to talk about

    *   what emotions are associated with each situation they listed (don't try to make it better);
    *   whether or not it is OK/normal to have these feelings;
    *   how people normally deal with difficult situations (for them) and the consequences;
    *   whether or not there is anyone in the group or team for whom emotions are not a problem, and what skills or strategies they use to deal with problematic situations.

4. Finally, ask people to pair up with someone who has complementary strengths, if possible, and draw up a strategy of what they might do, think, or feel differently next time, based on what they have shared and learned from each other. (10–15 minutes)

Activity 21 Family Drama

Facilitator Notes

This exercise is designed to give people an insight into learned behavior and emotional competence and help them identify any emotions that, for whatever reason, are taboo or uncomfortable for them (in that person's history). It can be a challenging exercise and will require a high-trust group environment. It also needs to be sensitively managed because participants may become defensive about their past or their families. For this reason, it is better for the work to take place in pairs and for each pair to have a choice about what they feed back to the whole group. The learning is more personal than in most group activities, although the behavior that is permitted (or not) in the whole group might be different after the activity is run.

(continued)

Activity 21 Family Drama (*concluded*)

- Working in pairs, participants recall a drama or crisis that has happened within their immediate family or an argument they have had recently with a partner or relative. They describe the situation they are remembering and explore with their partner the qualities of the drama. If the behavior and feelings being expressed were seen through a camera lens, would it be described as a tragedy, a comedy, a soap opera, or a pantomime? (10 minutes per person)

With their partner, participants should reflect on these questions:

1. Which soap opera, Shakespearean play, or situation comedy does your scenario most resemble?

2. Does the scenario give you any clues about which emotions were acceptable to express in your family and which were not? (For example, in my family, anger was not allowed, but humor was—so every drama turned into a situation comedy of sorts!)

3. How do you feel as you look back on the family drama from today's perspective? Do you respond in the same way to such dramas as you did then? Are there some feelings that are now acceptable and others that are taboo?

Coaching

When you are helping someone be more effective in managing their emotions, it is important for them to understand which emotions they have difficulty with and why. Often there will be patterns of thinking and old tapes running that go back to cultural or family situations connected to certain emotions. Work with the coachee on the following questions:

1. How do you feel when another person becomes angry, distressed, fearful, joyful?

2. How do you usually behave when this happens in a group you are leading?

3. What rules do you have about the expression of emotion in groups you work with?

4. How do you stop yourself from expressing emotion as you are feeling it (mentally and physically)?

5. What fears and anxieties do you have about becoming angry, fearful, or intimate in a group?

6. Think of times when you have seen people you respect managing their emotions well, and consider what they do that you can learn from.

It will help the coachee if together you identify the next situation when they will have an opportunity to better manage their emotions. Knowing that they will be reporting back to you will enable them to stay focused on the behavior they want to change (or the different interventions that they can use).

Facilitator Self-Development

1. Identify and become familiar with your own physical responses to the following emotions:

   - anger
   - sorrow
   - joy
   - fear

2. Place a ✓ next to each word or phrase you are most likely to use.

   ☐ I think   ☐ that makes sense

   ☐ I understand   ☐ let's get this straight (mentally identified)

   ☐ I agree

   Note: People who lead with their mind (thinking) might always seem to be in control, but might lack passion, warmth, or energy in their decision making. The challenge if you relate to this is to allow yourself to have an emotional response and allow some of the emotion to be reflected in decisions and behavior.

   ☐ I feel   ☐ that feels right

   ☐ I believe   ☐ let's sit with this for a while (emotionally identified)

   ☐ I hear

   Note: If you are somebody who leads with your feelings, you may want to slow down and take time to think before you act in response to your emotions.

3. Practice accepting and valuing your own feelings—those you like and those you do not like.

4. Explore with a supervisor or friend what the worst thing would be for you if you became angry/sad/afraid/happy in the groups you were facilitating.

5. Read *Working with Emotional Intelligence* by Daniel Goleman.

1.9 Skillful Challenge

If you are facilitating, it is imperative that you know how to challenge others and deal with difficult behavior. This activity builds trust in a group, promotes openness, and encourages people to bring more of themselves into their work.

Your task as facilitator is to give people permission to express their fears and anxieties during the session and provide a safe environment to do so.

A common mistake made by facilitators is to be personally offended by difficult behavior. This can then lead to power struggles and facilitator loss of confidence in his or her abilities. The team or group might also lose confidence in their ability to achieve their task.

A useful model for understanding what happens when challenge takes place in groups is shown below.

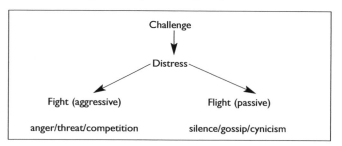

When we are challenged or threatened, we typically experience distress. This raises our adrenaline levels and brings into play the well-known fight/flight response:

- Fight responses involve attacking as a means of protection. This is where people become angry, threatening, or highly competitive.

- Flight defenses are passive, characterized by avoidance. Some people will stop listening; others will become gossipy, jocular, or cynical.

If you are facilitating, you have to know your own typical reactions to challenge. Do you avoid challenge? Try to compromise? Or enjoy the emotions that challenge arouses? The key for the facilitator is not to be fazed by challenge, but to draw up a contract so that you and others have boundaries that make everyone feel safe.

If you are challenged, take it out with the whole team or group. If what you are doing isn't working, ask for a list of concerns and suggest another approach, or ask the team for suggestions. Again, make sure that you get agreement with the team before moving on. Remember that the facilitator can only work if agreement has been reached.

It is also useful to bear in mind some of the common causes of challenge:

1. *Motivation.* Why are people there? Do they feel they have any influence over what is happening? Is their challenge born out of frustration, or is something else going on? Acknowledge what you see and hear and don't try to dismiss it or suppress it, because it will resurface in another way. Try to raise people's awareness and responsibility of what they can change, rather than what they can't change.

2. *Expectations.* Check what expectations people have of the team or group. Some people will have high expectations and others low expectations. If people are feeling disappointed about the team or group, they may decide to vent their frustration by challenging your authority. Remember, however, that people have to take responsibility for their own expectations.

3. *Hidden agendas.* Think about whether or not there is anything else going on that is provoking the challenge. For example, is there an unresolved or unidentified conflict in the group? Look out for indirect attacks. Is anyone being scapegoated? Gauge the atmosphere—what are your senses or your instincts telling you?

4. *Reframing.* Instead of labeling behavior as difficult, try to see it as offering you useful information. A group of civil servants once dealt with change by cracking jokes all the time. They were avoiding their own feelings of powerlessness over the proposed personnel cuts in their department by using humor. It is often useful to look at behavior and see if you can "reframe" it before reacting. Remind yourself that quiet people sometimes lack confidence, that critical people are typically perfectionists who are hardest on themselves, that garrulous members are afraid of silence, and that people who tend to blame others often don't know how to take responsibility.

Perhaps most of all, remember that when you challenge others, don't try to prove a point or try to win. What you should be doing is highlighting behavior that isn't working, and making participants aware of other strategies that are more productive.

Activity 22 Nice Price

Facilitator Notes

This activity focuses on the consequences of NOT challenging others to be honest and open with their true feelings. The intent here is to raise awareness and get participants to challenge one another.

1. Ask participants to pair up and consider which of the following statements are true, and then assess what the consequences are.

   - If I'm seen as too nice, people won't give me open or honest feedback.
   - If I don't tell someone off, they will never learn.
   - If I'm nice all the time, I deprive someone of seeing who I really am.
   - If I'm nice all the time, I deprive myself and others of my passion.
   - If I'm nice all the time, I will come across as self-righteous.
   - If I'm too nice, I may lack drive and ambition.
   - If I'm nice all the time, people will use me. (20 minutes)

2. Draw out the group about the "cost" of being too nice, and what the alternatives to being too nice might be. How fearful are they of not being nice enough? (10–15 minutes)

Activity 23 Difficult People

Facilitator Notes

This activity is designed to empower teams or groups, build trust, and find practical strategies for dealing with difficult behavior.

1. Ask participants to list all the behaviors that they find difficult to deal with in groups or meetings. Divide the group into small groups of three or four and have each group choose one of the behaviors listed and do the following:

   a. Discuss that behavior, providing real or hypothetical examples of how it manifests itself.
   b. Explore strategies for challenging that behavior.
   c. Consider what the consequences of that challenge might be, positive and negative. (20 minutes)

2. Ask the small groups to present their findings to the whole group. Ask for further input from the other groups if any particular behavior is especially difficult. Trust the resources of the team or group to know what strategies will work. (5–10 minutes per group)

Note: During feedback, share your ideas, but don't feel that you need to provide a "right" answer. This exercise is empowering for groups because they are releasing fears and anxieties and realizing that other people have similar fears. Some people will resist the exercise initially and want the answers from you. Hold your ground and encourage participation. A volunteer can document the findings as a handout for the group.

Activity 24 Conflict Resolution

Facilitator Notes

This is an intervention that deals directly with conflict in a group. The underlying concept in this model is empathy—the ability to put yourself in the shoes of another person and see the world from their perspective.

1. If there is a direct conflict between two team members that is getting in the way of the task at hand, it is best to take some time to try to resolve the conflict. Ask the people concerned if they are prepared to work toward reconciliation. If they agree, have them listen to each other and try to understand both positions.

    This intervention can be done with others (the two people sit in the middle and the rest of the group observe as they sit in a circle around them). If they are not prepared to talk in front of the whole group, then offer the group something else to do.

2. Invite the people involved in the conflict to sit opposite each other. Ask the first person to start by taking 5 minutes to talk through the issue as they see it.

    Participant A talks without any interruption from B. Participant B then summarizes what he or she has heard until A is satisfied that B understands the issue from his or her point of view. (10 minutes)

3. Repeat this process with B talking and A listening and summarizing. (10 minutes)

4. Invite them to physically switch places and each take 5 minutes to talk about the issue as if they were the other person. (10 minutes)

5. When they have each done that, ask them to sit back in their own seats and take turns stating where they are and how they feel about the issue in the light of all they have heard. (10 minutes)

6. Now ask them if they can see any way forward or any solutions to the differences between them. Let each person state their new position, without interruption; they should say what they are prepared to do differently. If they are still deadlocked, they each need to take a larger perspective. Ask them to consider what they need to do for the sake of the whole team. (15 minutes)

7. To complete the process, ask them to agree on what they are going to share with the group. Gain a commitment from them that they will each honor and from which they will not deviate without consulting each other first. (5–10 minutes)

Coaching

Identify with your coachee those situations that might push him or her into fight/flight behavior. Which of these are most problematic? Discuss with your coachee the strategies that they might use to deal with such behaviors.

As a coach, you will also have plenty of opportunity to model compassionate challenging. Remember that in your role, you are simply acting as another pair of eyes and ears for your coachee—you aren't better than your coachee or necessarily more experienced than they are, but you can share what you know. Your attentiveness to the situation is all-important: If you hear something that isn't right or notice something that they are avoiding, challenge them on what happened. Raise your coachee's awareness about what happened and ask what action or role they took. The best challenge sometimes feels like no more than reassessing a situation together.

Facilitator Self-Development

1. Reflect on any behavior that you find difficult to deal with.

   - Explore the effect that the behavior has on you and how you responded.
   - Ask yourself if this behavior reminds you of anyone with whom you have had difficulties in the past.
     —If the answer is yes, write down in detail what their similarities and differences are. Be very detailed in your description of the differences (looks, mannerisms, voice tone, body language, etc.).
     —If the answer is no, explore ways to respond should that behavior arise: positive self-talk, inviting another group member to respond, vowing to hear from two more group members before addressing the behavior, working out a contingency plan, and so on.
   - Have an organizational supervisor intervene if the problem persists, because you don't want to be held hostage to this kind of behavior.

2. Reflect on your ability to challenge others.

   - Ask yourself this question: *When do you have a right to confront others?* Write down your answers.
   - Write down the worst things that could happen if you challenge someone's behavior and it all goes wrong.
   - Write down the best things that could happen if you challenge someone's behavior and it all goes right.
   - Consider what help you might need from others if you challenge someone's behavior.

3. Practice assertiveness daily.

1.10 Facilitating Feedback

We are all pretty familiar with the idea of feedback. It is a well-established management technique. Most people have a broad understanding of the importance of feedback and understand how to give and receive it, but this doesn't mean they do it well.

Feedback is scary. We sometimes feel uncertain about our right to tell people what they are doing well and what they are doing badly. How will they react? What happens if they don't like the feedback we give them? Does it lead to more problems?

It is also hard to accept feedback. It sounds like criticism, which makes us get defensive. After all, what right has anyone else to highlight our weaknesses when they have plenty of their own? It can make us angry if we feel that the person giving us feedback is doing so not to help us, but to expose our faults.

These are fears every facilitator must address, because feedback is a technique that you have to be adept at. As a facilitator, you will need to be able to challenge behavior, notice individual and group dynamics, and support and value colleagues. Feedback has to be part of every facilitator's toolkit.

At the outset, the facilitator and manager need to concern themselves with the following types of feedback:

1. *Positive feedback.* We all like validation, but it is often harder to praise someone than to find fault. Some managers say that they don't praise their staff because they fear that it will unleash immediate demands for a raise in pay. Praise, far from being something to resist, is something that all managers and facilitators should be generous with because we all like to be appreciated.

   Facilitators should enjoy praising workers for their effort and successes. How do you give positive feedback? It is more than a pat on the back. You must highlight a specific piece of work or activity, and detail what particular aspects of the work you think made it so successful. Such praise doesn't have to be accompanied by a song and dance, but rather treated as something normal and expected.

2. *Constructive feedback.* Let's say a colleague is preparing for an important presentation and they ask you to sit in for a rehearsal. With constructive feedback, you recognize both what went well and what might be improved. It is not about you and what *you* might have done—it is about noticing the details about the other person's performance so that they can adapt to the requirements of the situation.

   Constructive feedback is based on a nonjudgmental and positive regard for the other person. Feedback is given to encourage the other person as well as to highlight specific areas of behavior or actions that might need changing. In such a case, the neutral offering of alternative suggestions can be a helpful form of feedback.

3. *Challenging feedback.* Feedback is not about criticism, nor is it a veiled opportunity for one-upmanship. It is about highlighting performance, behavior, or actions that are not working or that are unacceptable or not up to standard.

   As a facilitator or manager, you will need to challenge some people, but you do not need to do so in a hostile way. Be clear, raise awareness, and establish where responsibility lies. To be able to challenge someone else, you will, of course, need to have a clear contract (see

Activity 14). This might be the company rules and regulations, team contracts, or performance standards. If you don't have a contract in place, you might find that the ground you stand on is rather shaky.

Remember, we give feedback to someone else for their benefit, not ours. It is used to draw people's attention to the consequences of their actions. It can help them see things more clearly or do things more effectively. Sometimes it is about giving information and about appreciating their worth.

Finally, it is worth remembering that feedback is a two-way process. As a facilitator, you have to be prepared to "walk your talk." Ask for feedback from your managers, your colleagues, and your team. Without this information, how will you know if what you are doing is effective?

Activity 25 Feedback Review

Facilitator Notes

This is an exercise to introduce the subject of feedback and to help people assess what skills they already have. This activity can be useful for people who are training to be facilitators, as well as for managers and teams who want to develop clearer methods of communication.

1. Ask the group or team to divide into pairs and to consider the guidelines below. Ask them to choose either the Giving Feedback checklist or the Receiving Feedback checklist and think of a situation where giving feedback or receiving feedback might be useful. (10 minutes)

2. Ask them to describe the situation to their partner and to consider which of the guidelines in the checklist might have priority for the situation they have in mind. Ask them also to assess how these guidelines might make a difference in how they give or receive feedback. What are the traps they normally fall into? (20 minutes)

    Feedback is useful for appraisals, project reviews, day-to-day management, disciplinary interviews, group or team situations, training scenarios, coaching, supervision, and meetings.

Feedback Checklists

Giving Feedback

1. Choose an appropriate time and place, and make sure the recipient is ready to hear what you have to say.

2. Maintain communication. Use feedback as an opportunity to listen to what the other person has to say, too.

3. Describe, don't judge: feedback is not the same as criticism. Feedback should be neutral. Describe the facts and let the other person draw their own conclusions.

4. Be specific. "The way you asked John for his suggestions really opened up the discussion" is more useful than "you handled that meeting well."

5. Focus on your reaction to behavior, and try not to blame. "I notice how hard I find it to make my opinion heard" is far better than "You talk so much, I can't get a word in edgewise."

6. Distinguish between the person and their behavior, and avoid commenting on characteristics that can't be changed, such as accent, personality, or appearance.

7. Be constructive. When giving challenging feedback, provide alternative suggestions.

8. Try to offer feedback as close to the event as possible.

9. Care about what you say and how you say it.

10. Check for understanding and reaction.

(continued)

Activity 25 Feedback Review (*concluded*)

Receiving Feedback

1. Remember that you don't have to accept feedback—it might not be true. However, bear in mind that it can provide you with useful information from which you can learn.

2. Be open, not defensive. Feedback isn't criticism. Try to make the most of the situation.

3. Listen well and maintain dialogue. Don't react until you are sure what the feedback is. Then reply. If you don't understand the feedback, ask for clarification or a specific example. Seek specific suggestions for doing things differently.

4. When receiving negative feedback that you think is true, accept responsibility for it without denial or apology. Don't beat yourself up for getting things wrong. We all make mistakes, and it's one of the best ways to learn.

5 If the feedback you are given isn't justified, reject it calmly and factually and ask the feedback giver how they arrived at that conclusion.

6. Enjoy giving positive feedback.

Activity 26 Who am I to you?

Facilitator Notes

This exercise can be used to help trainee facilitators and employees learn about the process of self-assessment and how to give and receive feedback. Before you start this exercise, you must make sure that participants understand the principles of giving and receiving feedback.

1. Make sure that people have read up on the principles of giving and receiving feedback, and go over best practices for giving and receiving feedback. (10 minutes)

2. Ask all the participants to prepare to look at how they see themselves. Some of the issues that they might want to consider are self-esteem; how important their "image" is to them; how it has changed; how they are usually perceived; and when they make the most effort with others. (20 minutes)

3. Ask people to form triads (or small groups). Participant A begins by assessing themselves, prompted by Participant B (who acts as the facilitator). Participant C (and any other) acts as the observer. It is important to stress that there are no right or wrongs here and no judging. The person who is speaking must be as honest as possible in his or her self-appraisal. Participant B's task is not to engage in the discussion, but rather to paraphrase what he or she hears, ask open and probing questions, and, where appropriate, prompt for details. (10 minutes)

(continued)

4. Feedback is given to Participant A by both B and C. It should focus on A's self-appraisal, including what strengths and weaknesses A mentioned, how this self-assessment came across, and how they assess A's image: Is A's self-appraisal one that they share? This feedback should follow best-practice guidelines (see Activity 25 checklists) and needs to be written down by someone other than Participant A.

   Note: For those who are not familiar with the feedback process, one of the proven forms of giving feedback is the "sandwich" technique. In this technique, you start off by providing feedback on what you saw or heard that was a strength. Then you provide feedback on something that you feel could be improved that the participant might not be aware of. Finally, you state again something that you appreciated or enjoyed. (5 minutes)

5. It might be best for Participant A to give B and C a few minutes to reflect on the feedback and sift out what they want to "take on board" and what they don't. However, if they are unclear about the feedback or want more clarification about particular traits, then allow some time for that, too. (5 minutes)

6. Now Participant A observes, B becomes the speaker, and C facilitates. Repeat the process until all participants have assessed themselves and been given feedback. (15 minutes per person)

7. Bring the whole group back together and see if there were any common themes, specific learnings, and practical difficulties. Consider, too, the applications of feedback. When can feedback be of real benefit? Examples here are coaching, appraisals, interviews, communication, meetings, and learning situations. Also discuss with the group whether or not it is okay for someone to say that they don't want feedback. (15 minutes)

Coaching

Coaching is an ideal time to give someone positive and constructive feedback. People like to be recognized and appreciated, so look for opportunities to praise people for specific things they have done. This will establish a valuing relationship and a valuing working culture.

As coach, you can also provide challenging feedback to someone about work they have completed that hasn't gone well, or behavior you've observed that doesn't seem to be working. Don't make judgments, because you will only rile the coachee or make them defensive. Simply raise awareness of the specific behavior and help the individual understand their personal responsibility for the situation they are in. Remember: It is the behavior you are challenging, not the person.

Facilitator Self-Development

There are countless opportunities to give feedback. At work, for example, there are formal settings such as team meetings, appraisals, and coaching situations. There are also many situations outside work where you can practice giving informal feedback. Many businesses ask directly for feedback from their customers on the phone, through questionnaires, or through consumer research. These are ideal situations to build up your skills.

Asking for feedback can be more daunting. We might not want to hear what people really think about us—good or bad. However, it is worth remembering that feedback is just good communication. It helps us get a clearer view of how we are behaving and how well we are doing. With this in mind, here are some ways to build up your skills:

1. Give feedback to yourself. Use a diary or journal to reflect on a particular job, encounter, or project, and notice what you did well and what you might need to improve. With a journal, you can be completely honest, so don't be afraid to brag or to be critical. Remember, however, to focus on both positive and negative aspects.

2. Ask your manager to give you feedback at the end of the next project on which you work.

3. Read *The Complete Feedback Skills Training Book* by Sue Bishop; *Communication in Management* by Hargie, Dickson, and Tourish; and "Give and Take" in *Management Skills and Development* (October 1997). Many books on performance management, counseling, and mentoring have sections or chapters on feedback.

4. There are some interesting off-the-shelf games on feedback. "The Feedback Game" by Peter Gerrickens is available from Gower, and "Giving and Receiving Positive Feedback" by Peter Garber is available from HRD Press, Inc.

PART TWO

Group and Team Facilitation

2.1 Group Process: Inclusion

Facilitators must know how people behave and interact in groups. To do this, we need to look at what people set out to achieve a task, and how they get along—the processes of group activity.

People often behave quite differently in groups and teams than they do in one-to-one settings. Some people become quiet, some turn into bullies or tormentors, and some become jokers. For the facilitator who has to rely on others to get the job done, this can be daunting. Why is it that a meeting feels electric one moment, and awkward the next? Why do some people refuse to communicate, while others do all the talking?

It becomes easier to understand if we look at a practical example. Imagine that you are in a team meeting and two people start arguing. Do you feel embarrassed? Do you try to stop it? Do you join in? When people work together in groups, all sorts of things go on: allegiances are made, cliques are formed, feelings are acknowledged or overlooked, reactions are triggered—and all this makes up the group dynamic or process. If we try to pretend it doesn't happen, doesn't matter, or is inappropriate for the workplace, we are fooling ourselves: such behavior is the lifeblood of the group or team! The facilitator who develops an understanding of how groups really work is in the best position to help the team overcome any difficulties.

A model by Will Schutz is helpful here. Schutz used three simple words to sum up what takes place in team or group dynamics at a deep level: inclusion, control, and openness. (See the diagram on the next page.)

This section and the following two sections explore these issues in more detail and give ideas for interventions that will help facilitate the group process in the areas of inclusion, control, and openness.

Inclusion

Schutz's first dimension in his group process model is inclusion: whether or not group members feel significant and to what extent they feel included or excluded by colleagues. In teams where there is scapegoating, one or more individuals might be either shut out by colleagues or will exclude themselves in some way. Another example of inclusion is when new members of a team are excluded for lengthy periods of time, perhaps because they are perceived as being a threat to the status quo, or when they are quietly resented for daring to replace someone who has left.

Inclusion and exclusion issues are typically unspoken and form part of a hidden agenda that may not even be in the consciousness of the people involved. For example, in one training group, a new member joined the course and appeared to be welcomed by his peers—lots of introductions and smiles. However, the group then proceeded to make witty asides and share private jokes, excluding the new member. In this kind of situation, the facilitator should consider drawing the attention of the group to its behavior.

You might sense that something is wrong but not know what the problem is or where to begin to address it. Groups often aren't aware of their behavior (or it is covert). A skilled facilitator heightens their own awareness so that they can pick up on the behavior of group members that is impacting the whole group.

How do you become more aware of what is really going on? You may pick up on feelings, thoughts, or body sensations, or have an intuitive insight. This level of communication is part of the magic of facilitation; it requires practice, trust, and objective detachment. The focus is about using all our resources, wherever they come from, and putting them to use in order to serve the group, typically by making interventions about the ongoing process.

When it comes to inclusion and exclusion, the facilitator should notice and be aware of the variety of ways people in groups attract attention or interest (and in so doing, make themselves more prominent). The group joker, for example, might want to stay safe (hiding behind humor) as well as to gain recognition. The underlying interpersonal fear here might well be a fear of being ignored and feeling insignificant, unimportant, or worthless. Although their external behavior is very different, the same underlying fears they are protecting themselves from can apply to individuals who are silent or withdrawn in a group; they are protecting themselves from being ignored by maintaining their distance, privacy, and self-sufficiency.

Inclusion has to do with interacting, seeking attention, acknowledgment, recognition, status, identity, and individuality. It is unlike openness in that it does not involve strong emotional attachments to any individual. It is unlike control in that the preoccupation is with prominence in groups—not dominance.

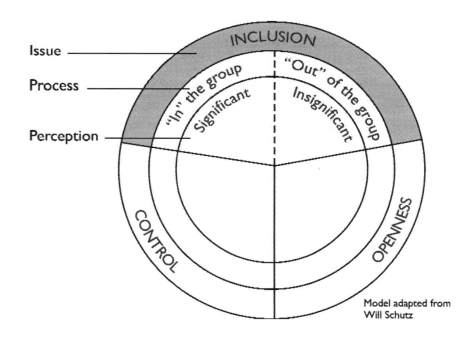

Model adapted from
Will Schutz

Activity 27 Understanding Inclusion

Facilitator Notes

This activity about inclusion best suits people who, from a learning styles perspective, are theorists or reflectors. It provides participants with a framework for understanding inclusion before you ask them to consider and share their own experiences. Use this activity also to help teams understand team performance issues, to provide insight into group dynamics, or to develop strategies to deal with inclusion/exclusion problems.

1. Introduce the theory and the model on page 66. (10–15 minutes)

2. Discuss the need for confident interaction in all teamwork situations, sales meetings, appraisals, consultancy interventions, customer service situations, and so on. (5 minutes)

3. Discuss the reality that there will be people who do not feel part of a team. (5 minutes)

4. Consider why people feel significant or insignificant in a team or group setting. Likely topics to surface here are trust, need for attention, feeling valued, sense of belonging, safety, communication, under-achievement. Prompt if necessary. (10 minutes)

5. Ask the group to consider the case of a team that loses one or two of its key players. Get the group to brainstorm circumstances in which a team might include or exclude new employees (for example, not introducing themselves, not sharing information, making private jokes). (10 minutes)

6. Ask people to discuss in pairs one or two experiences they have had when they felt excluded from a group or team, and what impact this had on them. If they can't think of any personal experiences, ask them to share their observations of individuals who have been excluded from a group or team. (10–15 minutes)

7. Draw together the whole group for discussion. The point here is to get participants to be aware of inclusion and exclusion as a reality in teams. If people are excluding others (or themselves), team performance will be affected. Consider, with the group, appropriate strategies for dealing with such individuals, such as making an appropriate challenge, valuing people, or drawing attention to the issue. (10–20 minutes)

Activity 28 Rope Tricks

Facilitator Notes

This is an experiential exercise best suited for people who, from a learning styles point of view, are activists or pragmatists. It uses the theme of "space and boundaries" to illuminate how much contact people like, need, or are used to. Use this activity to help team players understand what they bring to the team, highlight the dynamics of contact between people, and build awareness about effective team performance.

Materials required: For this exercise, the facilitator will need to use lengths of thick string or thin rope (one 6- to 8-foot length for each participant) and a flipchart.

1. Introduce this exercise briefly and tell participants it will help them explore team dynamics. Explain that you will help make sense of the experience afterward. Give people permission to try things out and experiment, and remind them that there are no right and wrong answers. (5 minutes)

2. Ask the group or team to split into two groups (A and B). Give each participant a length of rope or string and tell them to arrange the rope around themselves so that it expresses how much space/contact they like to have with or from others. Give them time to try this out. (10 minutes)

3. Ask individuals to look at where the others have placed their rope and respond accordingly. Explain that they can always adjust it when the situation demands. As facilitator, you might want to pose some questions here, such as these: What would it be like for people to make more or less contact? How do other group members respond to you when you move your string or rope closer? How do you respond when other people make moves toward them? Which people are easy to make contact with? Where are they most comfortable? Most uneasy? How do they determine what moves to make? (15–20 minutes)

4. Next, tell the groups that there has been a team reorganization. Select a member from Group A to join Group B, and vice versa. Ask both teams to rearrange themselves with their lengths of rope in response to this change. (10 minutes)

5. Draw up some questions on a flipchart for people to consider, and get them to discuss them in their groups. Relevant issues for people to consider here could be:

    *   What did you notice about your own and others' need for space and contact?
    *   How significant did you feel in your group?
    *   Did you experiment? If so, what was the outcome?
    *   What was your reaction to the change in group personnel? (15 minutes)

6. Help the group make sense of the activity by introducing key aspects of the theory. Use Schutz's model to highlight the issues of significance, encounter, and feeling "in" or "out." Make links between these and group effectiveness. Ask the group for comments, and see if there are any insights.

    Consider, with the group, appropriate strategies for dealing with people who are either being excluded or who exclude themselves from group participation. Such strategies could include making an appropriate challenge, valuing people, and drawing attention to the issue. (15–20 minutes)

Coaching

If you are coaching someone on how to manage groups or coaching a team member who is having difficulty feeling part of a group, highlight exclusion and inclusion. Ask your coachee if he or she has had experience with either one. If not, present the model to make them aware of team or group dynamics.

You might also ask the coachee to share their own insights into who is "in" and who is "out" of the team. Ask them how they feel and how they react to the people who are "out." Your objective here is to help the coachee become more aware of what they are doing (or not doing) to help the situation.

Remember, it is your responsibility as a coach to support and value the coachee, not to take responsibility for them. With encouragement, most people can find their own answers. Ask them about their own personal experience in teams and groups, and help shed light on those areas where they seem most stuck. Don't try to determine what is right or wrong behavior, but highlight what you see as the consequences of their actions. Remember that genuine support and appropriate challenge lie at the heart of coaching.

Facilitator Self-Development

If you are facilitating others on the subject of inclusion, you need to know your own history and patterns. The key attribute that the facilitator needs here is awareness. If you haven't explored your own past, a group will see this or will resist your suggestions. In effect, they won't trust you enough to share what their own feelings are on this subject. The following suggestions can help you to explore your own issues of inclusion:

1. Write a story of your own experience in groups. Be as creative as you want to be. Include photographs, pictures, and family myths. You can also write a straight biography about the most-important groups you have been in, how you felt when you joined them, and what role(s) you found yourself taking. If possible, take the time to explore this approach with your own coach, mentor, or counselor.

2. Read *Joy: 20 Years Later* by Will Schutz; *Truth or Dare* by Starhawk; *The Red Book of Groups* by Gaie Houston; and *Group Counselling* by Keith Tudor.

3. Ask a friend or colleague who is good at listening to ask you these questions:
   - What role do you normally take in groups?
   - How do you include and exclude yourself in groups?
   - Why do you facilitate groups?
   - What are the subjects you prefer to explore with groups? Why?

4. Ask for honest feedback from your partner, your best friend, your mentor or coach, or someone at work who has seen the way you interact in meetings. Ask them to say what they thought when they first encountered you in a group setting, and whether or not they saw you taking any particular role. Alternatively, ask them to describe with three adjectives how you behave in groups (for example, "Anna is challenging, domineering, and clear thinking").

2.2 Group Process: Control

When people are together in a group or team, they have to work out for themselves how to get along. This is the second dimension in Will Schutz's model of group dynamics, and it is all about how much control we feel that we need or want or exercise.

Control has negative connotations for most of us. We don't generally want to be seen as out of control and we don't generally like control freaks. We also tend to resist being controlled. Yet in groups, the issue of control will quickly emerge as people struggle for power. Not everyone will want to dominate, and some will feel incompetent and fear responsibility. Such people can be loyal followers, but organizations increasingly want people to be able to make decisions, to think on their feet, and to take charge of situations. Being too much of a follower isn't helpful.

The polar opposite to this is when people are excessively domineering. Take the example of the person who always wants to win, who always thinks their ideas are the best, or who undermines other people in meetings by speaking over them, ridiculing them, or subverting the process when someone else is talking. You may have been in a meeting when suddenly someone starts a separate conversation with a colleague or even leaves the room to make a quick call on their cell phone. What they are actually saying by such actions is "I am the only one worth listening to. Don't pay attention to anyone else." There are many ways in which people bid for power, and not all of them are immediately transparent; some people are happiest as kingmakers, rather than as kings. In such cases, the need for prominence is low, but the need for control is extremely high. The outsider in the team or group will be operating similarly with unresolved inclusion issues and high control needs.

If an individual takes over as leader, the chances are that someone else will be looking for opportunities to cut him or her down to size. If these bids for power are ignored by the manager or facilitator, there is a real chance that people will take sides, and the team or group will be seriously diverted from its objectives.

There are also real dangers when people try to share power, but haven't worked enough on their interpersonal relationships. For example, at one conference, two workshop leaders decided to co-run an event. They both knew their material, but they had different presentation styles. It quickly became clear that there was little tolerance for each other's priorities. Whenever one would start to speak, the other would butt in with a differing opinion or insist on having the last word. Although they weren't aware of it, both leaders had unresolved control issues. As a result, neither they nor their audience got what they wanted.

Facilitators should always expect control to be a problem for someone. They must know how to manage it when it does arise, such as bring the domineering behavior to the attention of the team or the individual. Threatening emotions, bullying tendencies, and manipulative actions should all be addressed by the facilitator; the facilitator doesn't need to be hostile; indeed, if the facilitator ends up in a battle for control, nothing will be resolved.

The facilitator needs to maintain their objectivity and be looking for genuine ways in which they can change the behavior of the person who wants control. The facilitator can explicitly state that they want views or contributions from everyone. They can acknowledge the forthright opinions of the autocrat, yet still encourage cooperative rather than competitive decision making.

The same attitude of care and concern needs to be extended to the abdicrat. (An abdicrat is someone who *abdicates* all responsibility for decision making.) If people are anxious or feel threatened in groups, it is up to the facilitator to create safety and to demonstrate that everyone's opinion is valued. By encouraging people to work in pairs, the facilitator can make sure that people who are naturally reticent will participate.

It is worth remembering that labeling people as autocrats or abdicrats (or anything else) is to stereotype them. Knowing that this person is domineering and that person is submissive can make us feel better, but it is seldom as simple as that. All people are fallible, all people have off days, all people get triggered by things people say or actions they take—including you. You have great power, but it is how you use it that counts. Remember that the facilitator's role is to serve the group—to help people take responsibility for their own and the team's performance.

Activity 29 Understanding Control

Facilitator Notes

This activity is an approach to control that will best suit people who, from a learning styles perspective, are theorists or reflectors. It provides participants with a framework for understanding before you ask them to consider and share their own experiences. Use this activity to help individuals within teams to understand how much they contribute, how they contribute, and what responsibility they feel they have to the group.

1. Introduce the theory and the model below. (10–15 minutes)

2. Discuss the subject of control in relation to teamwork, meetings, consultancy interventions, customer service, and so on.
    Discuss how people might be domineering in a team by talking, showing off, having to win all the time, subverting others, or arriving late. (5–10 minutes)

3. Discuss how people might opt out of a group by being quiet, not taking responsibility, always deferring to others, not negotiating, or not confronting. (5–10 minutes)

4. Divide the group into two and ask the first group to consider the case of a team where some people never contribute. Ask the second group to consider the problem of some people being overbearing. Get each group to brainstorm examples of likely behavior and ways in which they could respond either as facilitators, managers, or colleagues. (10–15 minutes)

5. Draw together the whole group for discussion. The point here is to raise awareness that control is linked to issues of competence and responsibility and that it is a natural part of team behavior. The key is to take responsibility and make decisions when we need to, as well as to build competence. (10–15 minutes)

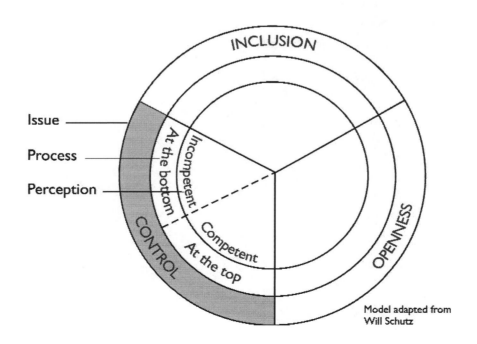

Issue

Process

Perception

Model adapted from
Will Schutz

Activity 30 Power Line

Facilitator Notes

This activity highlights the creative power of the continuum. You can use the technique to help people see what control problems they have with other people in the team or group. This exercise is especially useful for people who are training to be facilitators.

1. Explain to the group that the purpose of this exercise is to examine what happens in the dynamic process of the group by "freezing" how we are thinking and feeling now.

2. Ask the group to imagine a continuum or line of power whereby one end of the room represents the most power and the other end represents the area of least power. Tell the group that they must place themselves along that line, depending on how much power they feel they have.

   Note: There will be a great deal of concern about this exercise. Some people will jostle for the top-dog position, while others will surrender or pretend not to care. Some people might feel very unhappy. It is the facilitator's role to contain the group, observe, and remain objective. (5–10 minutes)

3. When the team or group has finally settled into place, go to the person at the top of the continuum (the most power) and ask them what it feels like to be there. Ask them what they notice about other people in the line: Is it what they expected?

   Now, ask the person at the bottom end how they feel, whether or not they like being there, and where they might wish to be. Check with others to see how they feel in this continuum. (10–15 minutes)

4. Ask the person at the other end of the continuum to rearrange the line either as they see it or as they would like it to be. Again draw out comments. (10–20 minutes)

   Note: It may well be that the team or group asks you, the facilitator, to place yourself on the continuum or arrange it as you see it. If you are an ongoing member of the team or group, it might be important for you to act as a member of the group and to model authenticity. If, on the other hand, the group is looking to you to resolve their differences of opinion, it might be better not to act as one of the group. Being clear why you are using this activity will help your choice here.

5. Allow the group to take a break after this exercise. Then bring them back and discuss what they have noticed about themselves and others. Highlight any dynamics—especially concerning people who tend to either dominate or disappear. Be nonjudgmental with your observations. (15–20 minutes)

Activity 31 Thumb War

Facilitator Notes

This is an exercise that can be used either as a warm-up to the subject of control or as a less-provocative alternative to the Power Line activity (Activity 30).

1. Ask participants to pair up and hook the fingers of their right hand with their partner's fingers so that their right thumbs are on top.

2. Instruct participants to jump their thumbs over each other three times and then, keeping their fingers hooked, try to pin the other person's thumb down for a count of three. (2 minutes)

3. Ask participants to talk about how competitive they got, what strategies they used, and what they felt when they pinned down someone else or were pinned down. Did they find it fun? (5 minutes)

4. Then ask participants to pair up with someone they don't normally work with or someone they see as opposite to themselves. Repeat the exercise. Then ask people to discuss how the exercise went and why they see the other person as they do. Be prepared to facilitate the process. (10–20 minutes)

Coaching

When coaching someone on control, explore the subject of competence—not only the actual competencies they see others demonstrate at work, but also how they feel about their own level of competence. If people feel competent, there is less need for them to have to control others.

Another way to look at this issue is to focus on styles of leadership. Winston Churchill is often held up as a model of great leadership, but he had an autocratic style. When is autocratic leadership useful? When is it not? What would it be like to be in a team where an autocratic leader was in control all the time? What happens to the team dynamic?

If you are coaching an abdicrat who leaves power to others, focus on how he or she can take more control. Perhaps this individual is unwilling to take responsibility. Work with your coachee on what support he or she needs to take more control and what fears he or she has about taking responsibility. Also talk about the appropriateness of an autonomous style of leadership. When is it right to be hierarchical? When is it right to hand over responsibility to others?

Facilitator Self-Development

If you are helping others with control, you need to start with your own feelings of competence. Check to see how easy or difficult it is for you to let the team take responsibility for its own tasks and processes. Also check to see how easy or difficult it is for you to manage with sole authority and control.

The following suggestions can help you explore your own issues of control:

1. Observe yourself the next time you join a new group in or out of work. Notice how much responsibility you want to take and how much others take. Observe other people's competence in relation to the responsibility they take. On paper (and for yourself only), draw a power line continuum of the group and notice where you have placed various people on that power line.

2. Make a list of the people in your team who have more power than you and a list of those who have less. Don't just think of status. Note where you place yourself in terms of power in the team, and reflect on where you'd like to be.

3. Check with your partner or closest friend about what things you take responsibility for, and why. Is it a shared load? Or are there some areas where you would like to give some control back? If so, what support, if any, do you or they need in order to take or give up responsibility?

2.3 Group Process: Openness

According to the theory of Will Schutz, there are three dimensions to human interaction. First there is the *inclusion* dimension when people meet or encounter each other. Then there is the *control* dimension, where people work out how to get along together. The third dimension in Schutz's model is that of *openness*, and it is in this phase that the crucial ties of trust and affection are formed.

It is no surprise that many leaders are putting trust at the top of their agenda. High-performing teams are built on trust; many managers recognize that with the pressure and responsibility placed on teams, they need in return to promote trust as a central tenet of working practice. However, openness needs careful handling, and trust needs to be earned. Think back to a time when you were last in a team: What happened when someone asked a näive question or admitted to something that had gone wrong or proposed a new idea? How did you and the rest of the team respond?

In the culture of many organizations, one of the first things that people learn to hide is their vulnerability. It is all too easy to destroy new ideas with cynicism. And despite the widely accepted view that we learn best from our mistakes, most people feel that failure is more likely to be punished than rewarded.

However, if you are looking to build a robust, cohesive, and effective team, this issue of openness is crucial. It might sound counter-cultural to the way businesses have traditionally operated, but in today's empowered, customer-focused workplaces, organizations need people who can make decisions, take responsibility, and feel supported by their colleagues.

For facilitators working with openness, the issue of relationship is core. Are people in the group or team accepting of others? Is it safe for them to ask for support? Do they openly share their concerns with others? Or are they more typically closed in their work relationships?

For individuals, the underlying dynamic here is whether or not they feel they are liked. If, at a deep level you do not like yourself and do not want others to see just how unlikeable you are, you might well try to avoid relationships with others.

Of course we all have behaviors, characteristics, or memories of past experiences that we'd rather keep private. Openness isn't about flinging open the doors of your personal history and expecting total and immediate acceptance. Rather, it is about developing an understanding of how you operate with others in team or group environments. Once we have a greater understanding and awareness of our own strengths and weaknesses, we can be more accepting of others.

It is worth noting that people who avoid relationships are not the only ones who can benefit from working on openness. Some people in groups and teams are popular or friendly with everyone, but some of these individuals are actually guarding against any meaningful contact. In effect, their relationship with others is superficial.

Try not to be overly personal with someone who has openness issues. You may have come across people who want to tell you everything about their feelings as soon as they meet you. They might be trying to relieve their anxiety by asking for your complete approval and acceptance. Such behavior is manipulative, and can often produce the opposite reaction from that desired: such needy behavior will often drive people away.

Facilitators working with openness need to remember that they can't make people like each other. It's something that has to happen in its own time. The model, however, is useful; it gives people permission, often in very sterile working environments, to be more interpersonal. If the team or group is at the forming stage, the facilitator can highlight openness as a necessary condition for effective group work and establish a dynamic and open team culture.

If the team has already formed, you might still use the model, but also look together at how openness is displayed in the team by, for example, drawing the team's attention to how they do or don't support each other and how much they share about their learning experiences. Encourage the team to develop listening and observation skills and appreciate their differences. You'll find them encouraging one another to be more open.

It is a basic human need to be accepted and trusted. Facilitators will be working with the flow. Remember, the point here is to encourage people to express and receive appropriate and positive feelings—not to get them to reveal their darkest secrets.

Activity 32 Understanding Openness

Facilitator Notes

This approach to openness best suits people who, from a learning styles perspective, are theorists or reflectors. It provides participants with a framework for understanding before you ask them to consider and share their own experiences with openness. Use this activity to help teams understand team performance issues, to provide insight into group dynamics, or to develop strategies to deal with the expression or denial of appropriate feelings.

1. Introduce the theory and the model below. (10–15 minutes)

2. Discuss the need for confident expression of feelings in, for example, teamwork situations, sales meetings, appraisals, consultancy interventions, customer service, and so on. Discuss the practicality of relationships within a team. How important are they? (5–10 minutes)

3. Consider the issues and outcomes for people who avoid relationships in a team or group. Likely topics to surface here are trust, fear of intimacy, the presence of emotion in a business culture, self-esteem, and feeling like an outsider. Prompt if necessary. (15–20 minutes)

4. Ask the group to consider the case of a team where people never relate to one another. Get the group to brainstorm examples of appropriate supporting strategies (for example, "I'd like to hear more from X," coaching and mentoring strategies, and this sharing of personal difficulties). (10 minutes)

5. If the team or group is ready, ask people to share in pairs something of themselves that they don't normally talk about at work. It doesn't have to be a great secret, but it should be something of personal significance. Instruct one of the pair to ask why it's hard to talk about this at work, and ask the other to listen. After 5 minutes, they should each paraphrase what they have heard.

   Draw together the whole group for discussion. The point here is to raise awareness in people that openness is a powerful aspect of team behavior and that, in being open, we help others and help ourselves. (10–15 minutes)

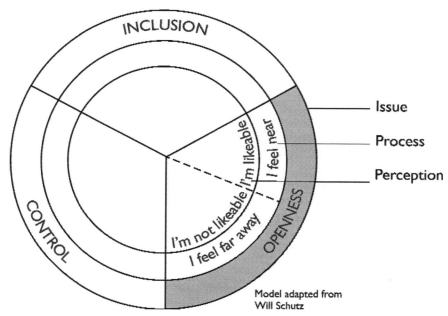

Model adapted from
Will Schutz

Activity 33 Three-Legged Search

Facilitator Notes

This is an experiential exercise. It highlights issues of interdependency, support, and authenticity. Use this intervention to help team players see how they relate to one another.

Materials: For this exercise, the facilitator will need to use strips of cloth or ties (one 2-foot tie for each pair) and a flipchart. Participants should be given the opportunity to leave the room and find or collect an object or possession.

1. Introduce this exercise briefly. Tell participants it is a two-part, paired exercise to help people explore issues of openness. Say that you will help them make sense of the experience afterward. Ask participants to pair up. Explain to each pair that during the next 20 minutes, their task is to discuss as truthfully as possible how well they work together, what their strengths and weaknesses are, and what their relationship might look like from an outside perspective. Instruct the pairs that their task is to find and bring back an object (or pair of objects) that might represent their relationship.

2. Now, additionally, explain to each pair that they will have to conduct this exercise with their legs tied together as in the traditional three-legged race. Ask people to notice what emotions they felt during the exercise, what difficulties they faced, and how they overcame them. Give a strip of cloth or tie to each pair.

   If you are using the break time for this exercise, let the pairs help themselves to refreshments as they work. (20 minutes)

3. Once they have reassembled, invite the pairs to introduce their object and explain why they chose it. Prompt them, where necessary, to talk about the difficulties they faced and whether or not they enjoyed the forced intimacy of the exercise. (15–20 minutes)

4. Help the group make sense of the activity by introducing key aspects of the theory. Use Schutz's model to talk about acceptance, trust, feeling open or closed, and so on, and link these things to team effectiveness. Ask the group for comments, and see if there are any realizations or insights.

   Consider with the group or team appropriate strategies for dealing with people who avoid relationships or who are over-personal. Such strategies could include drawing attention to the issue, providing feedback, and offering support. (15–20 minutes)

Coaching

Start coaching someone on openness by asking the coachee some questions. What sort of relationships do they have with their colleagues? How do they manage feelings at work? When might they think it is appropriate and inappropriate to express feelings?

If you, as coach, are dealing with someone who might need to work on the issue of openness, explore the subject of emotional intelligence (EQ) with your coachee. There are psychometrics available that assess EQ, but you can encourage the coachee to do their own exploring around the subject. If they need some prompts, suggest some of the references that follow.

The hardest thing for some people is to praise or value other people; others find showing their vulnerability far harder than, say, giving someone critical feedback. Yet most of us crave recognition and long for meaningful relationships and are especially critical of the workplace for being so emotionally barren and critical of managers for overlooking all the work we put in. As coach, you can model what it is like to be open by expressing your feelings, by noticing the contribution your coachee is making, and by challenging negative cultural norms.

You might also ask the coachee to give their own insights into their own team. Which members seem to be more open? How do they know? What are the signs, and what effects does being open have on other people? Your objective is to help the coachee become more aware of themselves and others.

Facilitator Self-Development

If you are facilitating others on the issue of openness, you need self-awareness. Imagine asking your team to do something that you can't do yourself; clearly, they would be reluctant or even hostile to the idea. The challenge for facilitators is to explore their own relationships. Remember, facilitation isn't about being perfect or knowing all the answers. It is important, however, to be authentic and congruent.

The following suggestions can help you explore your own issues of openness:

1. Think of some of the groups you have been in. How long does it take you to form close ties? If you had to go into a new group tomorrow or go to a party where you don't know anybody tonight, what strategies would you adopt? Try not to censor your thoughts. Think about how open you are to others.

2. Read *Emotional Intelligence* by Daniel Goleman, *The Truth Option* by Will Schutz, or *Chicken Soup for the Soul* by Jack Canfield.

3. Ask your closest friend or partner to write down and/or tell you what your best qualities are. Then do the same for them and notice how you felt in both cases.

4. Take something in to work that is personal and that represents who you are or what you believe in—a side of you that you don't normally show. If possible, try to include this side of yourself at work. Be prepared to take a risk in showing a more open side of yourself. Notice how people respond.

2.4 Understanding Roles in Teams

Groups are the basic units of society within which we grow, learn, socialize, and work. Each of us has a lifetime's knowledge about how groups work, yet many people are unproductive in group settings.

Because so much of our work as facilitators is done with teams and groups, we need to understand core group dynamics and know how to guide groups through difficult group situations.

There are three aspects in team or group work that facilitators must keep in mind at all times:

1. the aims and objectives of the group
2. the working relationships among group members (which make up the group dynamic)
3. the changing needs of the group as it matures

These elements are ever changing and sometimes conflicting, which makes the role of facilitation so necessary, demanding, and exciting.

Task and Process Roles

The roles members of the group play affect tasks and relationships.

- *The information provider* brings knowledge that is illuminating for others. The danger here is that sometimes they provide too much information.

- *The questioner* dares to ask about issues that others are reluctant to raise and challenges given assumptions. However, their questioning can become destructive.

- *The clarifier* teases out meaning in relation to the aims and objectives of the group by checking understanding. However, over-use of clarification can be frustrating and delay the group.

- *The initiator* tends to want to get the ball rolling, and brings energy and initiative to the group. However, they can lose focus on the problems because of their tendency to keep the group bouncing along with new ideas and activities.

- *The concluder* pulls contributions together and summarizes what has been happening for the group. However, make sure they don't close down discussion prematurely and fail to listen to all contributions.

Relationship and process people have their negative dimensions.

- *The third eye* (or *observer*) will typically stand back from the group dynamic and make an observation about what is happening to the group as a whole. This helps the people involved see where they are stuck and make an appropriate shift. However, such people can spend too much time watching others as a defense against participating fully in the group.

- *The encourager* demonstrates support verbally or nonverbally. This is clearly of great value to some members of the group, but facilitators need to be sure that encouragers don't make a habit of automatically supporting opposing views or generating hostility for never saying where they stand.

- *The comic* brings light relief and cohesion to the group and helps ease tensions. However, the comic can also become the group clown; fooling around can undermine the group and become a subtle way to put others down.

- *The discloser* is someone who shares their experiences and thus deepens the group process, engendering trust. However, beware of the discloser who dominates the group with their personal agendas or whose inappropriate sharings simply cause discomfort to others.

Facilitators may want to consciously adopt some of these roles in order to bring insight, humor, or energy into the team or group. However, the facilitator does not have to be an expert in all these roles. They will have their own favorite roles (and group members will also have theirs). Just be aware of which roles people are taking in the group at any given time, value people for the qualities they bring, and understand how to challenge with awareness.

Activity 34 Picture Boxes

Facilitator Notes

The intent of this activity is to raise awareness among participants about the roles that they naturally take in the team or group. The task will occupy them enough not to be self-conscious during the exercise. Beware, however, that if the group dynamic is negative, it will be harder to complete the task, and group members may blame you for this or believe that you have tampered with the process in some way.

Materials: You will need six chunky children's jigsaw puzzles (each with about 6 to 10 pieces) for this activity. However, two of the jigsaw puzzles should be exactly the same—there should be only five different pictures in total.

1. Mix up all the puzzle pieces in a colorful box and invite group members to each take a handful until all the pieces are taken. Invite the group to then get on the floor (if possible) and do the puzzles. Tell them that two of the puzzles are the same. If the group is cooperative and positive, it should take about 10 minutes for the task to be completed.

   Note: The activity tends to accentuate the roles that people take because it will remind people of childhood or school experiences.

2. Observe during this time the different roles that people adopt (see theory).

3. Once the pictures are completed, ask the group to debrief. Ask them to ask themselves these questions:
   - What role did they take? Was this role familiar?
   - Did they feel pushed or tempted to take another role?
   - Who are they allied with? What role did that person take?
   - What roles did other people take?
   - Were they task-focused? Or process-focused?
   - Did they react to any particular behavior? (10–15 minutes)

4. Draw out the key points regarding task, process, and roles, and explain that it is quite normal for people in groups to jostle for position. Ask the participants this: Are you aware of your actions and motivations? When are individuals helping and not helping the group as a whole to achieve its task? (10–15 minutes)

Activity 35 Truthful Communication

Facilitator Notes

One of the ways to understand a group's dynamics is to look at its interpersonal communication. Some people choose to ignore what others are saying, while others change the subject, interrupt, or start making asides. The goal of this activity is to look at what makes up effective interpersonal communication in teams and groups.

(continued)

Activity 35 Truthful Communication (concluded)

1. Write on the flipchart the "Truth Option" below:

    - If I choose to tell you what I am aware of, I am being honest.
    - If I choose to tell you something contrary to my awareness, I am lying.
    - If I choose not to tell you something I am aware of, I am withholding.

    (Source: Will Schutz, The Truth Option, 1984)

2. Facilitate a group discussion about this statement. If people need some facilitative questions to start the ball rolling, suggest some of the following:

    - Is it always fair to tell the truth?
    - Do people have a right to know the truth?
    - What gets in the way of telling the truth?
    - What do you think/feel when you know people have lied? (20 minutes)

    Alternatively, ask people to reflect for 10 minutes on Schutz's statement and to consider how often they tell the truth, how often they lie, and how often they withhold. Then facilitate a discussion on what emerges. (15 minutes)

3. Ask people to form two small groups:

    - Group A should consider the impact of telling the truth on trust and open communication within the team.
    - Group B should consider the impact of *not* telling the truth on trust and open communication within the team. (15 minutes)

4. After they have considered their views, they should present them back to the whole group and see what is emerging.

    Note: There is sometimes disagreement on how much truth people think that others can bear, so set a clear time limit on discussions. (5 minutes)

5. Discuss appropriate and inappropriate ways in which people can tell the truth in teams. (10–15 minutes)

    Note: Blaming and judgmental statements often start with "You . . ." While they may be true, they are often seen as hostile or loaded, and consequently don't help communication. "I" statements, on the other hand, are about taking responsibility. ("I find it very uncomfortable when you don't say anything in meetings" is better than "You always rely on me to do all the talking in meetings").

6. Facilitate a contract with the team or group on clear and effective communication. Some of the people should agree on what each of these terms means:

    - "respect for others"
    - "honesty"
    - "constructive" (criticism, etc.)
    - "openness" (no hidden agendas)
    - "nonjudgmental"
    - "confidentiality" (where personal information is shared) (15 minutes)

Coaching

A "geneogram" is a model of family relationships that helps us see relationships and interpersonal dynamics clearly. Such models are increasingly being used in organizations to help people understand the organizational dynamics and personal relationships in the group and make sense of the role they play.

Use the following symbols for drawing up a "family tree" of relationships at work:

- a circle to represent a woman
- a square to represent a man
- straight lines between two people to represent a strong relationship
- dotted lines between individuals to represent a broken relationship
- a straight line with two slashes through it to represent a rocky relationship (for example, an argument or someone having left the company)

Always help the coachee start the tree and build the connections outward to link important or significant people at work. Once you have a graphic representation, talk about the coachee's relationship to each person and the history of that relationship. Use the information to go on to discuss if there are any patterns of behavior at work that are similar to those of the coachee and those of real family members.

This method is a way of highlighting areas of difficulty. It permits questions around key relationships and helps you and the coachee examine them more closely and look at helpful and unhelpful patterns of behavior.

Facilitator Self-Development

1. In schooling yourself to become more aware of group dynamics, use the following checklist in meetings to hone your observation skills:

- Contributions: Who contributes, who is silent, who talks to whom, and who keeps the ball rolling?
- Influence: Who talks and is listened to? Who is low/high in influence? Who competes? Who holds the power in the group?
- Decisions: How are decisions made? Are they usually the will of one person? Is there consensus? How are minority points of view dealt with? Who supports whom? Who is ignored?
- Atmosphere: What is the mood of the group? Is conflict suppressed or avoided? Who provokes and who defends? Do people seem involved and interested? Is the energy high or low?
- Membership: Who is included and who is excluded? Are there any pairings or sub-groups? If there were rules for membership of this group, what would they be?
- Feelings: What feelings are present in the group? Are there any attempts made to block the expression of feelings? If so, how is this done and by whom?
- Norms: What are the spoken and unspoken rules in the group? What is taboo for the group? How open is the group about how people work together? How much energy is put into the "grapevine"? Does the group adhere to any ground rules?

2. Work with a group that will make you think about who you are and how you get along with others.

(continued)

Facilitator Self-Development (*concluded*)

3. Observe families working together, and try to distinguish roles and norms, and who influences whom and how.

4. Watch the films *Twelve Angry Men* or *Lord of the Flies*.

5. Take a Myers-Briggs Type Indicator assessment with an accredited trainer.

2.5 Facilitator Authority

To be successful in facilitating, there needs to be an awareness of how power works in groups. Group members will look to you for leadership, regardless of the position you hold in the organization. The role of facilitator is invested with authority by the organization and by the people you are leading. It is important that you as facilitator recognize how and when to use the authority you hold.

There are times in the life of a group when a facilitator needs to use all their authority, fully and intentionally, to serve the group. There are other times when the facilitator needs to hand over power to the group. How and when you make this decision is key to your success as a facilitator. The qualities of awareness and flexibility are critical!

There are three bases of authority in facilitation. Bear in mind that we each use all three of them, and need the ability to move seamlessly between them.

1. *Authoritarian style (autonomy)*. As the facilitator, you direct the structure and content. You exercise all the authority provided by your role as facilitator, and you lead from the front; that is, you think and act on behalf of the group.

    The *strength* of this style is that people know where they stand. The *weakness* is that it is not likely to include or encourage contributions from all group members. A facilitator must "own" their power. There will be times when they need to instruct group members; if they are not comfortable with their authority, they will not be able to provide clear leadership and structure for the group. A facilitator who only feels powerful when in complete control will have a tendency to cling to authority to help

them feel safe and secure. The likelihood here is that they will end up engendering frustration and resistance to change.

2. *Cooperative style (cooperacy)*. This mode is characterized by an intention to include all group members in making decisions about how the group is going to operate. This power-sharing approach enables you to work with the group, guiding it to become more self-directing.

    The *strength* of this style is that it gives real power to group members, which, in turn, is likely to energize them to achieve their task. The *weakness* is that when mishandled, this facilitation style can leave group members unclear about who is in control, causing frustration. Facilitators who fear authority tend to want to work in this mode all the time. However, you cannot use the cooperative style until the group has formed and becomes clear about its aims and objectives, because it will only lead to confusion and uncertainty. The group will push hard to be led and will quickly lose cohesiveness if members do not feel they have a direction.

3. *Autonomous style (autonomy)*. This is where you respect the total autonomy of the group. You do not do things for them or with them; rather, you give them freedom to find their own way and exercise their own judgment without any intervention from you. Structure, content, and operation of the group is decided entirely by group members. You act as a hands-off guide.

    The *strength* of this style is that it harnesses the talents of all and encourages empowerment.

The *weakness* comes when the group actually needs more direction but the facilitator mistakenly lets it drift along.

Facilitators who avoid giving groups autonomy will miss out on the richness and resourcefulness of group members, but this style has to be used appropriately (e.g., inviting the group to break into subgroups or for project work).

Facilitation is all about knowing when to use which style. This chart will make it easier to remember which style is most appropriate as the group develops.

Group stage	Facilitator role per style
Forming and orientation Anxiety is high and group members do not know one another. The challenge is inclusion.	*Authoritarian style (hierarchy)* Take charge, break the ice, establish purposes and rules.
Storming and testing Group is working through individual differences. The challenge is control.	*Cooperative style* Support members, listen to all, observe roles.
	Authoritarian style (hierarchy) Manage conflicts, redefine objectives, be impartial.
Norming and settling Group cooperation develops. Focus is on task, open exchange of opinions, establishment of working methods. The challenge is openness.	*Cooperative style* Allow ideas to flow, encourage quiet members, hold the boundaries.
Performing and achieving Group is creative and hard working, meets its goals, works without guidance.	*Autonomous style* Allow group to manage itself.

**The Appropriate Mode of Authority
at Different Stages in Group Development**

Activity 36 Power Plays

Facilitator Notes

The aim of this exercise is to highlight the three facilitating "power" styles so that participants will know how to lead and be led by someone who uses each style.

Note: Preparation time 30 minutes; three sessions taking 30 minutes each (10 minutes facilitation and 20 minutes feedback/debrief).

1. Ask for three volunteers to role-play the three facilitator styles: authoritarian, cooperacy, autonomy.

2. Instruct the volunteers (and inform the group) that they will be exaggerating each of the styles. The exaggeration is important in order to produce a discernible impact in a short space of time. After each role-play, lead a short discussion on what it was like to be led in that style. The volunteers should observe the groups when it is not their turn to facilitate and feed back their observations to the group. (2–3 minutes)

3. Give the briefing notes, below, to the volunteers. Inform them that they will be leading the group for 10 minutes in the one style allocated to them. They can have 30 minutes to prepare, with support from you. They will need to choose a topic on which to facilitate that is appropriate for each style. (preparation time 30 minutes)

4. Tell the group members and the volunteers to be as authentic as possible in the role play. Remember that whatever feelings come up will be real. Note that the autonomous style can lead to feelings of frustration and aimlessness in the group, the authoritarian style may engender conflict or resistance, and that the cooperative style will probably feel the most comfortable for the group. (Facilitation 10 minutes, feedback 20 minutes per style.)

    Note: Start with authority and then autonomy, as these often produce the most powerful reactions. Cooperacy is a more grounding experience.

Briefing for Facilitator Styles

1. *Autonomy briefing:* You believe in letting group members come to their own conclusions about the issues under consideration. You see your job as getting the ball rolling and then providing the space for the group to discuss the topic with little interference from you. You are willing to let the discussion ramble because you believe that group members will be empowered if they can take responsibility for their own learning. You are there simply to provide them with a few triggers, but your favorite intervention is: ". . . and I am interested in what you/the group think about that." You think that much of the learning is in the exploration—that the journey, not the destination, is important. You allow periods of silence so that other members can make contributions. If directly challenged, you put the onus back on the group.

    Suitable topics for discussion in this style could be the environment, change, or social issues. If you want to make it challenging for the group, just allocate them 10 minutes to choose and discuss a topic. Beware that if you choose the latter, the group may well turn their frustration on you. If so, keep giving the topic back to them.

(continued)

2. *Authority briefing:* You believe you are an expert in your field and that you have much to say that is worth hearing. You also believe that you express yourself clearly and that, if group members take the trouble to listen, there is much for them to learn. While you are willing to allow some questions at the end of the session, you don't waste time by unnecessarily involving the group members. You believe that it is your job to provide information, advice, and guidance—and theirs to learn. You do not want too many interruptions, as you feel it breaks the flow. If you think there are too many people interrupting you, you will make a point of showing them who is in charge and whose session this is.

    To lead a group in this way, you need to choose a subject that you know something about (such as a hobby, a vacation destination, gourmet foods, or any other subject) that you can talk about with authority for 10 minutes. (It doesn't matter if the group is interested or not.) Think of strategies for dealing with interruptions so that you are not put off your stride (for example, say there will be time at the end for questions). Psyche yourself up for the role by thinking of a teacher you had in school who never listened to students.

3. *Cooperative style briefing:* Although you have a degree of expertise, effective leadership in this style relies on the group members being actively involved in the discussion. You see your role as drawing out the group's knowledge and understanding and blending it with your own so that all the resources in the group are utilized. This may involve sharing your knowledge of and commitment to the process. Your intention is to take every contribution of the group members seriously and attempt to blend them together to form a creative whole. Listening skills, paraphrasing, warmth, and acceptance characterize your style.

    In this style, exaggerate your interest in people's comments, agree with all points of view, and meet resistance with smiles. You want to be as inclusive as possible, so draw in quiet members of the group. Select a topic for discussion that you can open up to the group, and keep moving with open questions if the group gets stuck or falters (good topics: how to improve team meetings or what to do for this year's company get-together).

    In a debriefing session, ask the participants:

    - How did it feel to lead the group in that style?
    - How did it feel to be led in that style?
    - What impact did it have on you as a group member?
    - How did it affect the group dynamics?
    - What did you learn about that style of facilitation?

Activity 37 Dimensions of Authority

Facilitator Notes

One of the challenges for prospective facilitators to understand is which authority style to use in which situation. This activity asks people to reflect on the six core dimensions of facilitation.

1. Ask people to pair up and give them a copy of the boxed text below. Ask participants to take one or two of the dimensions and discuss when they would use these dimensions in real life and which authority style would be most appropriate. (10–15 minutes)

2. Ask the pairs to present their reflections/considerations to the group (5 minutes per pair). Facilitate a discussion aimed at highlighting the need for flexibility around authority. See if people are aware of their own personal preferences and which styles or dimensions are most difficult to apply.

---

1. *Planning*: The goal-oriented aspect of facilitation.

   With an authoritarian style, you choose for the group what they will do. Cooperatively, you would plan the event with the group. With autonomy, you delegate the planning, in whole or part, to the group.

2. *Meaning*: The cognitive aspect of facilitation having to do with understanding and making sense.

   The authoritarian makes sense of what is going on by offering your observations. The cooperative facilitator invites group members to participate with you in the generation of understanding. With autonomy, you give no views and let them make sense of it for themselves.

3. *Confronting*: The aspect of facilitation that has to do with challenge.

   Authoritarians interrupt behavior, highlight issues, and apply rules. Cooperative facilitators work with people to raise consciousness about issues that need addressing. With autonomy, you create a climate of trust so that challenge occurs independently.

4. *Feeling*: The aspect of facilitation that has to do with managing emotions.

   Authoritarian facilitators decide what feelings are appropriate. Cooperative facilitators prompt the group to share feelings and value one another. With autonomy, you give the group space to express and manage its own emotions.

5. *Structuring*: The formal aspect of facilitation that has to do with methods of learning.

   As the authoritarian facilitator, you will introduce exercises you've decided on. Cooperative facilitators structure the learning with the group and cooperate in its delivery. In autonomy, you give space for the group to devise and manage its own forms of learning.

6. *Valuing*: The integrity aspect of facilitation, where you build trust and rapport.

   The authoritarian makes statements about his or her commitment to others and their worth. The cooperative facilitator works with the group in a way that is founded on respect. With autonomy, you create space for the expression of individual and group self-determination.

The Six Dimensions
(adapted from John Heron)

Coaching

Explain some of the theory to your coachee, and model the different styles of facilitator authority with them. See if they are aware of their own preferred style and see if they can spot when they use different styles. When are these occasions? Are there some people with whom it is easier to be cooperative? Authoritarian? Autonomous? Raise awareness of the roles that the coachee takes in other groups. Leader or follower? Use the analogy of sports teams to unearth the profile of the coachee and see whether or not the coachee is a team player or a loner. How does he or she make decisions?

Discuss the styles of other leaders and managers. Sometimes managers tend to swing from being overly authoritarian to failing to take any responsibility for their actions or those of their team. Explore with your coachee how to build the involvement and commitment of their team.

Facilitator Self-Development

1. Reflect on your role in the family: Are you an organizer? Or do you let others organize you?

2. Read *Working More Creatively with Groups* by J. Benson, *Failures in Groupwork* by R. Coyne, *Group Dynamics* by D. Forsyth, or *The Horse Whisperer* by N. Evans.

3. Next time you are about to organize a birthday party, Christmas dinner, or vacation, see if you can organize it in a cooperative style. See who comes up with what ideas, and see if you can encourage others to take responsibility for them.

2.6 When and How to Intervene

As a facilitator, how do you choose what intervention to make? And having made it, how do you know it was the right one? The first-time facilitator will have many such questions, and they will not be easy to answer because facilitation is a style as unique to the individual as their personality and the way they express themselves. There are, however, some definite skills that the facilitator can develop that will help guide their interventions, as well as a number of clear principles for facilitative intervention.

First we need to remember that the purpose of the facilitator is to empower others. The facilitator has power, but is charged with using their awareness and responsibility for the benefit of the individual or group with whom they are working. Any intervention that the facilitator makes should be objective and nonjudgmental. For example, let's say you are aware that people on the team aren't saying what they are thinking. You decide to tackle the issue because you want an open working atmosphere. However, if participants think you have an agenda, they may resent your intervention or play dumb. The skill of the intervention is to act "in the moment" (when you are aware that something isn't being said) to highlight the issue in a nonjudgmental way by saying, for example, "I sense that people might have some strong views about this." Then you can suggest a structure (for example, looking at what can and can't be spoken about in the team) that would allow people room to explore the issue. As facilitator, you might help them see what effects withholding has on the team.

In facilitation theory, there are three kinds of interventions:

1. *Degenerate interventions* can be well-intentioned, but are misjudged, and are made when you are not aware of your own motivations or defenses. For example, you think that you are doing the right thing in trying to help people get along in a team, but you might be rather frightened of expressions of anger or conflict.

2. *Manipulative interventions* are made when you consciously want to manipulate the situation. For example, let's say you don't like someone in your team; you might deliberately try to shame them in front of their peers.

3. *Appropriate interventions*, as mentioned above, are made to bring awareness to the individual or the team. In some respects, appropriate interventions are rather like good parenting: there is great care and compassion, and suggestions are offered rather than imposed (or tough love is exercised to challenge behavior).

Core Skills

There are a number of core skills that the facilitator needs in order to be able to make appropriate interventions:

- *Listening.* Listen to the words, to the tone, to the hesitations. If you are managing a team, listen to what isn't being said as well as to whom is doing the most and the least speaking. Try not to make judgments about what is being said; instead, use your mind to evaluate the evidence and be prepared to summarize the key points.

- *Questioning.* As facilitator, you may think you know the answers, but if you want to empower your team, ask questions that help people come to their own conclusions. Questions can be used to probe, to open up discussion, and to challenge.

- *Speaking.* Too many people make the mistake of thinking that facilitation equates with being soft. It doesn't. As facilitator, you can be supportive, encouraging, and playful, but you can also be challenging, directive, and assertive. The requirement is to speak with impact and to believe in what you say.

- *Containing.* It is your role as facilitator to "hold the skin" of the team or group. You do this by being fully alert, moment to moment. By picking up all the clues from the team and by giving full attention to what is happening, you engender trust and establish the context within which you can make appropriate interventions.

The material in this manual is intended to help you build up your intervention skills, so be aware that this is just a starting point. Remember that interventions cannot be learned like a script; they come from your qualities (see Section 1.2) and your experience. Be flexible, trust your own resources, and remember your intent when intervening.

Activity 38 Pay Attention

Facilitator Notes

This activity aims to build awareness of the core intervention skills of facilitation. It can be used by the people training to be facilitators or with front-line staff who might need to facilitate meetings with colleagues or clients.

1. Ask the group or team to divide into groups of three. Explain that there will be a speaker (A), a listener (B), and an observer (C). Remind the team or group about the issues of confidentiality, and ask people to bring current concerns with them because this provides the genuine material that enables people to learn how to facilitate.

2. Ask the As to speak about a real difficulty they have been having with another person. This person might be within the working environment (not necessarily a colleague) or outside of work. If people cannot think of a person with whom they are currently having difficulty, ask them to remember an incident from their past. (5–10 minutes)

3. It is the task of the Bs to demonstrate active listening, to use questions sensitively to open up the issue, and to summarize the key points at appropriate times as A speaks. Instruct the Bs to look at how they contain the situation. How easy is it for them? What signals are coming back from the listener, verbal and nonverbal?

4. It is the task of the Cs to observe the As and the Bs, without interrupting. Instruct the Cs to look for what is and isn't being said and to look for nonverbal communication and emotional content, as well as factual content.

5. After the As have finished speaking, ask the groups to share feedback. For the As, what was their experience of being listened to? What was the quality of the listening like? Did they feel understood? Did they gain any insights? For the Bs, how easy or difficult was it to listen? What did they notice about their attention? What signals did they pick up? For the Cs, what did they observe in the As and the Bs about the quality of their interaction? (5–10 minutes)

6. Next, rotate the groups so that all participants have the opportunity to be speakers, listeners, and observers. (15 minutes)

7. Ask the team or group to come back together. Explore common insights and draw out examples of times when specific interventions are called for. (10–15 minutes)

8. For more advanced groups or teams, encourage the participants in this exercise to experiment with:
   - *Silence.* Ask the As on their own to observe a lengthy silence at one point during their talk and to observe how the Bs respond.
   - *Gestures.* Show the Bs how to practice becoming aware of their hand gestures and how to use gestures to accompany their questions and close down the As when their time is at an end.

Activity 39 Vacation Choices

Facilitator Notes

It is important for facilitators to be able to make "clean" interventions—interventions that aren't loaded or manipulative. This exercise is intended to help people make the distinction between interventions that are *degenerate, manipulative,* or *appropriate* (see theory).

- *Degenerate interventions* are made when you are not aware of your own motivations or history. Some of the red flags are poorly timed remarks, over-enthusiastic responses, talking over someone, over-assertive statements, and personal prejudice.

- *Manipulative interventions* are made when you consciously want to manipulate the situation. Signs of these types are inappropriate interruptions, belittling remarks, hostile comments, inappropriate use of status, and seductive manipulation.

- *Appropriate interventions* are made to highlight awareness or provide insights to a situation. They are relevant, well-timed, and perfect for the situation. Comments are nonjudgmental and suggestions are offered rather than imposed.

1. Provide some theory on interventions, and explain to the team or group that this exercise is designed to help them practice appropriate and inappropriate interventions. Make sure that the participants understand what *degenerate, manipulative,* and *appropriate* interventions are (see above). (10 minutes)

2. Explain to the group that this exercise requires Participant A to talk to Participant B (the facilitator) about a subject where there is some choice to be made (for example, deciding where to go for summer vacation). Someone from the team or group will sit behind Participant A so that they are only visible to Participant B. Furthermore, this person will have three large cards on which the words DEGENERATE, MANIPULATIVE, and APPROPRIATE are written. When the person sitting behind Participant A holds up one of the cards, it is Participant B's task to make the required intervention. The rest of the group will observe.

   At the start of the discussion, Participant B acts as facilitator while Participant A outlines the issues, their feelings about the situation, and the players involved in their vacation decision-making process. After a few minutes, one person from the group then holds up one of the cards, and Participant B is required to make the instructed intervention. The observers need to evaluate what impact the intervention had on the communication between the two participants and their ongoing discussion. After another couple of minutes, a group member chooses another card, and again Participant B has to make an intervention. Over a 10 to 15 minute discussion, Participant B should be instructed to do all three types of interventions. (10–15 minutes)

3. Following the exercise, ask for Participant A's feedback on their experience of being facilitated. Then ask for Participant B's feedback, and finally ask for the group's feedback. Once this feedback has been shared, try the exercise again with a different pairing. This time, choose another subject, such as "the next house I'll move into." (20–25 minutes per session including feedback)

Coaching

As a coach, you need to model how to make interventions, as well as to discuss and encourage your coachee to consider what interventions are most useful. Start by paying attention and using your listening, speaking, and questioning skills. Be directive, and suggest to your coachee that they build these skills into their personal development plan.

It is a good idea to explain how to make apparent the way the team or group interacts. The continuum activity is useful when there are a range of views in the team and you want to identify these views and explore what people feel about them.

In the activity, the facilitator creates an imaginary line across the room and suggests that one end of the line expresses one view and the other end expresses the opposing view. The facilitator asks people in the team to place themselves along the line according to the views they hold. The power of a structure such as this is that it manifests physically what is often hard to see. People can talk about their views, and people holding strong views can be identified. It is always easier to come up with possible interventions when the coachee has identified the issue. However, beware of your own bias and encourage the manager to use what they already know. Your trust in them will help them build their confidence.

Facilitator Self-Development

1. With interventions, it is strongly advised that you build up your experience. See how other people do it and see what activities you think work and which do not. Go to shows and exhibitions where expert facilitators demonstrate their skills, join a self-development group, or take some professional training.

2. The International Association of Facilitators publishes a newsletter and can provide information on helpful resources. Start off by accessing their Web site: www.iaf-world.org (also visit www.facilitationfactory.com).

3. "The Learner Within" is an interesting set of facilitator's materials from John Matchett Ltd. It is a card-based interactive learning resource designed to foster individual, team, and organizational learning. Founded on proven techniques in leading-edge management thinking, it contains models, frameworks, thought-provoking questions, suggestions, quotations, and resources.

2.7 Working with Diversity

Diversity is one subject many facilitators try to ignore by mentally filing it in the "too hard to do" basket. To work with diversity a group takes particular skill, sensitivity, and awareness. No matter how much you believe the groups you work with are homogeneous, the reality is that they never are. Differences can be subtle and invisible (such as religion or sexuality); they can be overt and obvious (such as gender, race, and accents); and they can be present but need stating in some way (such as class, ethnicity, belief systems, and values).

How many times have you attended team-building events that seem more like desperate attempts to get people on a team to work through their differences? Often what happens in such cases is that two or more team members can't seem to identify with the others in the group, creating a "them vs. us" situation.

The groups to which we belong form part of our self-concept. Belonging to an "in-group" becomes a place from which to compare and judge others (it makes us feel superior). Take the example of two people who constantly clash with one another, thus dominating team meetings with their constant carping, arguing, and disagreeing. A facilitator in one instance asked the team if they were prepared to explore the issue as a whole group, thinking that there was a problem the team was ignoring. They agreed and the team started to explore their differences. The list was lengthy: gender, sexuality, geography, background, life philosophy. But what was really blocking them from communicating was a mind-body split. One individual leads with his feelings (that is, he made decisions based on how he felt about things, and he was emotionally very

competent); the other person leads with his mind and actually distrusts his feelings.

Once the two realized that their basic communication styles were getting in the way of listening to each other and being heard, they were able to make changes. The rest of the team, who had observed the exploration process, felt able to talk about the differences they observed within the team and were able to be open enough to want to find another way of being together.

The key to any conflict is finding a bond or connection that can help us enjoy the differences in other people. Enormous differences emerge between friends or colleagues, but if the bond of mutual respect and trust is present, the differences can easily be accommodated. There is no doubt, however, that diversity in groups is complex and challenging, and there are no easy answers. Yet there are things you can do as a facilitator to promote openness, honesty, and good working relationships.

Encourage people to follow these six recommendations:

1. Develop ground rules together that will give a legitimate authority for members to challenge each other.

2. Make sure group members have the opportunity to interact with each other in a way that helps them discover whether or not some of their assumptions are inaccurate.

3. Be aware that situations that promote competition, produce frustration, or emphasize status differences strengthen, rather than reduce, prejudice.

4. Have an aspirational group goal that can be achieved only through cooperation.

5. Find stories (for example, Pokémon, *Lord of the Rings, Jason and the Argonauts*) that are all about the different qualities that each group member brings, without which the group as a whole could not succeed. Find out what qualities each group member has and why they were chosen for the team.

6. Bear in mind that the underlying issues in working with diversity are about power, inclusion/exclusion, and fear of the unknown. You don't have to clobber people with political correctness! Just look for ways to respect differences, learn more about them, and acknowledge them. Remind people that the ability to agree or disagree is paramount in groups, as it enables new perspectives to be drawn and frees up thinking and behavior.

It may be hard to find the confidence within yourself to venture into new territory. However, as a facilitator, it is important that you know your own level of tolerance and that, in any work where you perceive sharp differences in the group, you see that there is good supervision, coaching, and mentoring.

Activity 40 Little Boxes

Facilitator Notes

This is a pairs activity that will uncover some of the stereotypical beliefs and assumptions that we hold about one another. Use it to introduce people to the subject of diversity.

1. Ask people to pair up and to reflect for a few minutes on the questions below, writing their answers down before sharing their reflections with their partner. (10 minutes)

   - Question: What do you think is likely to be your partner's . . .
     —Favorite food?
     —Favorite type of music?
     —Favorite alcoholic drink?
     —Favorite non-alcoholic drink?
     —Favorite vacation destination?
     —Favorite pastime or hobby?
     —Favorite sport?
     —Favorite animal?
     —Ideal job?
     —Least-liked household task?
     —Ideal car?

2. The partner lets them know how accurate their answers are. After sharing their reflections, the pairs have a discussion about any assumptions that were made. For example, "When I first undertook this exercise, my partner assumed that my favorite food would be steak and apple pie, and that I would like rodeos and football. He made these assumptions simply because I am from Texas." (10 minutes)

3. Invite the pairs to debrief in the whole group, sharing any assumptions they had that turned out to be wrong. (10–15 minutes)

Activity 41 Pebble Power

Facilitator Notes

This is a simple but creative activity that encourages people to talk about their similarities and their differences.

   Materials: You will need a collection of 100–200 beach pebbles and a bag of colored marbles.

1. Place the collection of pebbles in the middle of the room, and ask participants to select a few. Don't give them any criteria for selection. (5 minutes)

(continued)

Activity 41 Pebble Power *(concluded)*

2. Ask participants to form small groups of three or four and to silently examine their pebbles together. Once they have done this, ask them to discuss the differences and similarities: what they like and don't like about the pebbles, whether or not there is anything about their shape/size/color that defines them as individuals, and so on. What qualities do they have? (10 minutes)

3. Now give each small group a selection of marbles (say, three per group) and ask them to put them with their group's pebbles. Ask people to notice what feelings and thoughts they had. Was this an easy and quick task? Who helped arrange them, and who held off? What were people's assumptions and judgments? What patterns did they create with the pebbles and marbles? (5–10 minutes)

4. Facilitate a group discussion about how we include people with differences. Do we judge ourselves? Do we judge them? How do we discriminate, and why? What are our personal limits of tolerance? (10–15 minutes)

Activity 42 Power Grid

Facilitator Notes

Diversity is not just about obvious differences between people. It can be much more subtle and hidden behind masks, roles, or status. This activity will encourage the group to be more overt about some of the subtle ways individuals try to influence each other and help them to be more aware of how they hide behind the different types of power they perceive themselves as having.

1. Introduce different aspects of power to the group using the grid and explanatory notes below. (5–10 minutes)

2. Now ask group members to discuss in pairs or threes how they would map themselves onto the grid in terms of the power they feel they have in the group and how they use it. For example, one group member may not have "physical" power, but uses their personal power to advantage in order to obtain the resources. Invite them to bring their examples back to the whole group. It may also be useful to ask the group to look at the different kinds of negative power they employ when the chips are down. This will give the whole group an insight into understanding that kind of behavior when it occurs. (10–15 minutes)

3. Open up the discussion about diversity. How do we use our differences? Do our differences hamper us? Or give us an advantage? Which aspects of power in the organization are most in demand? Which are least in demand? (10–15 minutes)

(continued)

Activity 42 Power Grid *(concluded)*

Types of Power

Personal	Physical
Political	Status
Professional	Negative

Power Grid Definitions:

- *Personal power* involves how we use our personalities, qualities, charisma, influence, and charm to achieve the task.

- *Physical power* is dependent on our physical presence and how we use our bodies, the space our bodies take up, and how we hold our frame (for example, in an aggressive stance or a submissive stance). Do we tower over others so that they have to look up to us? Or are we small, and thus feel intimidated a lot of the time?

- *Political power* stems from the resources we have at our disposal in terms of staff, money, skills, techniques, contacts, and so on.

- *Status power* derives from the position we have in the group or organization, and the power that is accorded to us because of that. How do we use it? Are we fair or unfair in the position we occupy? Are we pleased and content, or are we resentful at the position we are in?

- *Professional power* is the information we have—our expertise or knowledge on a topic. Are we willing to share it with others, or do we withhold it as a form of power? Do we gossip and let pieces of information slip every now and then so that people think we have more power than we actually do?

- *Negative power* is usually the resort of the people who feel least powerful in a group or organization. It includes manipulation, sabotage, cynicism, unhelpfulness, and any sort of resistance that undermines people or the task and makes "me" feel as though I had some influence.

Coaching

Coaching is, in itself, about empowering another person to achieve more and fulfill their potential. It is important to explore with the coachee areas where they feel different and discriminated against, and to identify times when the coachee does feel fully able to be who they are. What happens for them in that empowered state? How do they get into it? And how can it be anchored so that it is available to them more of the time? Take the coachee through some of the exercises outlined in this section. (See Activity 66 in Section 3.7, which helps people access their most resourceful and creative states.)

(continued)

Coaching (*concluded*)

Explore reverse coaching/mentoring. When Procter & Gamble wanted to address retention problems among female managers, the initial idea was to provide senior male managers as mentors to help them learn to think and behave in ways that might get them promoted. However, it was soon realized that the problem lay with the culture. The company decided to put the women managers into mentoring relationships with the executives. This made the women more visible. They learned about higher level decision making. It also sensitized the executives to a whole range of diversity issues.

Facilitator Self-Development

Here are some suggestions for building self-awareness regarding diversity and challenging your own assumptions and judgments.

1. Consider the following:
   - What opportunities have you had to learn about discrimination and diversity issues? Assess whether or not you may need to supplement your learning through further reading, courses, or supervision.
   - Be honest with yourself about the nature and level of power that you have and how you use it in society, at work, and in relationships.
   - Ask yourself if you can accept someone pointing out something that you didn't know about yourself.
   - Be clear about your level of knowledge and your skills, values, and experience, and how you currently help groups identify theirs.
   - Actively seek out new experiences and information that will help you understand different views of the world, other beliefs, and other cultures. Read *National Geographic* or any other journal that will expand your cultural awareness.
   - Be prepared to take risks, even though it will mean that you get some things wrong.
   - How do you challenge? Are you constructive and positive?
   - How patient and tolerant are you in attempting to resolve misunderstandings and complexities?

2. When working in groups, think about what ground rules you want in relation to behavior and language to ensure that group members are not excluded.

3. Have a contingency plan to deal with any direct or indirect discrimination in your groups.

4. Watch the films *Pocohontas*, *Blackboard Jungle*, or *Dangerous Minds*, which are about working with differences.

5. Find a way to break your patterns. Go to work a different way, try different food, make an effort to meet people with a different background, professional training, and perspective.

2.8 Working with Scapegoating

Scapegoating is one of the most pervasive and destructive dynamics in group life. It is therefore important to be able to recognize scapegoating and know what strategies you can use when it crops up in groups or teams.

We are all familiar with the concept of scapegoating from experiences on the school playground with bullying. Unfortunately, however, scapegoating is not confined to children and schools; it is also common in the workplace and has a powerful and negative impact on work and on morale.

What is *scapegoating*?

The scapegoat in a group or team is likely to be the individual who is perceived to have little power, who may well be seen as being different, or who least matches up to the group ideal. Scapegoats have lower perceived status than other members and are excluded in some way. For example, in working cultures where youth is consistently lauded, you will find that managers with years of experience (but a bit outdated) are ridiculed or ignored by younger staff members.

The way that scapegoating works is also pernicious: a group covertly agrees that all their difficulties, negative feelings, and defeats are the responsibility of one person, and proceeds to blame that person for all their problems. Usually the scapegoat is also invested with the qualities that people least admire in themselves, such as an inability to stand up to unfair criticism. The group's hostility is projected onto the scapegoat and becomes a basis for their solidarity—a "them vs. us" mentality that unites the majority against a common enemy.

The most common reason for the phenomenon of scapegoating is that some people fear confronting real and imagined differences in their team or organization. If a challenge to those differences is deemed to threaten perceived levels of cohesion, unity, and survival, the scapegoating process will occur.

Organizations and teams will not easily give up the well-worn pattern of blaming others for what they cannot do themselves. Consultants and whistle-blowers know only too well the dangers; the person who speaks the truth about the scapegoat often shares his or her fate. Consequently, the issue of scapegoating has to be handled sensitively.

Working with Scapegoating

Facilitators must not collude with those who criticize or gossip. On the contrary, they must be watchful for any behavior that resembles the scapegoating dynamic so that it can be challenged early. Working through scapegoating can achieve a level of group development in which diversity and collective responsibility prevail.

Scapegoating can have a number of causes. The fear of confrontation is one. The following are other causes that facilitators need to be aware of:

- abuses of power
- not enough listening or authentic communication
- failure to look at organizational or team "shadows" (*shadow* refers to the deeper, unspoken issues that lurk behind our consciousness and often unwittingly sabotage the group or team)
- a lack of management of diversity and differences within the team

- a weak management style
- lack of transparency in roles, responsibilities, and systems
- little or no self-reflection in the team or organization

It is important to remember that scapegoating is not a conscious choice; it is a dynamic that occurs in groups when people feel under threat for some reason.

A facilitator must be able to challenge the behavior of the group without evoking more defensive behavior that leads to them being scapegoated instead. The scapegoat represents the development potential of the group; to tap into that potential, the facilitator must refocus attention on a group's need for a scapegoat and its choice of victim, because it is a diversion from deeper collective issues. Hand back to the group the responsibility for what is happening and the part each member plays in the scenario. Establish firm ground rules for working together, which will help you foster an atmosphere of openness and curiosity about what may be holding back the team or group.

Once the group stops focusing on saviors, enemies, and victims, it can enter a new level of development and begin to value the contribution that each member has to make to the team effort.

Activity 43 · Dynamic Defenses

Facilitator Notes

This activity helps people understand scapegoating on a theoretical and practical level. The model provides a bridge to understanding. Getting people to move into groups helps them understand "typical" responses to stressful situations.

1. Outline the model below and invite participants to reflect on the roles that they resort to in times of stress. (10–15 minutes)

2. Ask people to choose and then move into provoker, defender, onlooker, and scapegoat groups. Once in these groups, ask participants to discuss with each other the positives and negatives of each role. (10–15 minutes)

3. Draw the group back into discussion and ask how people felt about these positions, how they can get stuck in these roles, and what the consequences might be when they do. (10–15 minutes)

The Model: A Briefing

This system model highlights four roles people tend to adopt when they feel threatened or are under stress. These are defensive positions, but they all have positive qualities. All these roles will impact on each other; when the team or group is not aware of the dynamic, it can get locked into negativity. Change does not occur when teams remain locked into negative positions. The trick, therefore, is to highlight people's awareness of their patterns, help them recognize the positive qualities in other positions, and help them choose to take responsibility for their behavior when they do feel under stress.

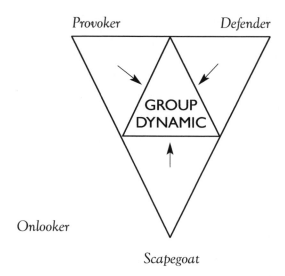

Dynamic Defenses Model

- *The Provoker.* The negative expression of this role will block all positive, creative, and innovative ideas expressed by others because they are threatening. The positive expression of this role is effective and honest challenging of ineffective modes or ways of working within the organization.

(continued)

Activity 43 Dynamic Defenses (*concluded*)

- *The Defender.* The negative expression of this role is to block the authentic challenges made by the provoker. This person has an investment in allowing the system to remain unchanged. The positive expression of this role is that when the provoker tries to scapegoat someone, the defender will protect the scapegoat.

- *The Scapegoat.* This role represents the powerlessness and negativity that is not allowed to be expressed within the organization because it is too threatening to success and unity. The scapegoat's part in the process is in accepting victimization. The positive side of this role is that if the organization can allow themselves to listen to the negative things that are being said, they have the opportunity to work through the fears and threats and have greater sensitivity and creativity to deal with challenges.

- *The Onlooker.* People who adopt this role can see what is happening, but feel powerless to intervene or may believe that if they do then they will be under threat themselves. The positive side of this role, however, is that they can provide crucial information about the dynamic in the team and contribute insight that leads to change in the team.

Activity 44 The Bomb

Facilitator Notes

This exercise helps prevent scapegoating by helping group or team members identify explicitly who in the group are their allies and who they find most threatening. It is a very active exercise, so facilitators need to be aware that it can raise powerful interpersonal issues. The room will need to be as clear as possible of furniture, bags, chairs, etc., so that there is plenty of room to move.

1. Ask the group to wander around the room and, while walking around, to mentally identify another person in the group who represents for them an unexploded bomb (whatever that means to them). Ask participants not to censor their first thought and to try not to rationalize their selection.

   Once everyone has had a short time to consider who this "bomb" is, ask them to move on a count of three, as fast as possible, to a position in the room that puts as great a distance as possible between themselves and their bomb. Notice where participants end up. (2–3 minutes)

2. Once participants have found their place, ask them to then come back to the middle of the room and to continue wandering around the room. Now instruct participants to mentally select someone in the group who represents a shield for them—someone who would protect them, defend them, or offer some reassurance. After a count of three, ask them to move as close as possible to their shield. Bear in mind that some participants may well have the same shield and that this can lead to mild chaos. (2–3 minutes)

(continued)

Activity 44 The Bomb *(concluded)*

3. Again, after participants have identified their shield, ask them to continue wandering around the room. This time, after a count of three, ask participants to place themselves in the room so that they have their shield between themselves and their bomb. Again, this typically causes some chaos and laughter because some participants will be considered bombs by some and shields by others. (2–3 minutes)

4. After a minute or so, while participants adjust and readjust their positions, ask them to freeze where they are. Then ask each participant to identify his or her shield and why (what qualities do they have), and identify his or her bomb and why. (15–20 minutes)

    State that one of the purposes of this exercise is to uncover the qualities that we put onto other people (such as "shields" and "bombs") that we have difficulty owning up to ourselves. If the group is willing, invite them at the end of the exercise to take back and accept the qualities that they share with others. For example, if we see someone else as dangerous, why is that so? What power are we finding hard to express that we can see so clearly in someone else?

5. This is a powerful exercise. Further debriefing can help participants process the feelings that have come up. Try asking participants to pair up and discuss what happened (for them) and how it relates to scapegoating.

Coaching

Explore with your coachee the model in Activity 43. What is their part in the positions in which they typically find themselves? How do such situations occur? What happens to their behavior when they are in this position? Is there anything they can do if they find themselves in this situation?

Explore with the coachee what they can do to help prevent scapegoating from happening in the groups that they are in or are running. Who are the most likely scapegoats (who they know)? Why? If the coachee can't think of any situations, ask him or her to think of situations in their past (or in the public eye). As coach, remember to ask open questions to help your coachee come to their own conclusions. You are there to prompt, support, and challenge; to highlight awareness; and to help build responsibility. Use models or examples to help your coachee make sense of the subject you are talking about, but stay objective.

Facilitator Self-Development

1. Find out about the history of the scapegoat.

2. Reflect on your style of communication with others during times of intensity or change in the groups or teams you work with. Try to estimate how much time you spend in each of the following modes:
    * judging (criticizing, bullying, comparing, complaining)
    * soothing (placating, mediating, seeing it from both sides, colluding)

(continued)

Facilitator Self-Development *(concluded)*

- avoiding (staying quiet, shrugging off responsibility, acting confused, changing the subject)
- rationalizing (lecturing, theorizing, quoting textbook cases, minimizing feelings)
- being assertive (leveling with others about what you think and feel, being clear, concise, and direct)

3. Watch the movie *The Scapegoat,* starring Alec Guinness.

2.9 Negotiation Skills

Whether you are contracting with the group, handling differences, or "selling" the task to the team, negotiation skills are an essential part of the facilitator's repertoire.

Much business and sports culture, however, is based on a win-lose approach. This can lead to:

- a stalemate between group members
- members interrupting one another
- members not listening to one another
- proposals being ignored, particularly from people perceived to have low status or little power
- pairings and power blocks being formed, which cause splits in the group.

Such behaviors are common, but they have damaging consequences: decisions get delayed, some group members become marginalized, and creativity gets completely blocked when win-lose behavior is not addressed. Furthermore, behavior like this typically pushes people into fight/flight response, which in turn leads to group members adopting either overtly hostile or defensive positions.

As facilitators, we need strategies to avoid such situations. If you want everyone to be a winner, everyone needs to understand that when people combine their creative energies, they most often achieve the best solution—a classic case of the whole being greater than its parts. You may well need some theoretical input to help the group so that people see what skills they are going to need to build, and why.

Individual negotiation skills

1. Regarding communication:

   - Make sure you know how to listen actively to others. Take time to understand the other person's needs, concerns, and desires.

   - Ask open questions beginning with what, where, when, who, and how (use "why" questions sparingly, as they tend to put people on the defensive).

   - Develop empathy, and be willing to look at the issue from the other person's point of view.

   - Be honest about what you want, and ask for it clearly and specifically. Help the other person understand how they can help you achieve what you want.

2. Regarding perception:

   - Don't allow your fears to push you into win-lose situations; deal rationally with the facts of the matter in hand.

   - Don't blame the other person for your problems.

   - Share and explore each other's perceptions of the situation.

   - Remain agreeable, and keep seeing the other person as a partner in solving the problem.

3. Regarding people skills:

   - Remember that negotiators are people. Treat them with courtesy and respect.

- Set a conciliatory tone.

- Talk about how you feel, and acknowledge and listen to how the other person is feeling.

- Do not settle for less than the right solution for both parties.

- Develop an ethical position. Stick to the principles of fairness, and value the other person's viewpoint.

Group Negotiation Skills

When negotiating with the whole group or mediating within the group, bear in mind the following:

- Use the agreed-upon goals and objectives of the group. Test out with the group the relevance of issues raised. Some issues will need to be "parked" until a later stage so that the task is not sabotaged. (Use a flipchart to record these issues to show that you intend to return to them.)

- Use yourself as a barometer of whether or not win-lose is creeping into group discussions. If you feel defensive or on the attack, you may be hooked into a competitive dynamic.

- Promote and reward collaboration by building on everybody's contributions.

- If there is clear disagreement within the group over an issue, invite participants to form a continuum where they stand along an imaginary line, with the farthest ends of the line representing the polar positions. This activity involves the whole group and gives everybody the opportunity to say why they have taken the positions they have. Allow everyone to speak, and invite participants to move up or down the continuum if their views shift. The continuum captures a physical picture of the issue and illustrates where energy needs to be focused.

Activity 45 What I Want

Facilitator Notes

This activity is focused on the limitations that people feel in negotiations. It also helps a whole group identify the personal "baggage" that they bring to the negotiating table.

1. Invite each participant to reflect on something they could ask of another participant ("I would like Brian to bring doughnuts once in a while" or "I would like Sara to review this handout/appraisal sheet with me to help me understand it").

    Encourage participants to take risks in thinking about what they want, even if they do not believe they will get an affirmative response. (5 minutes)

2. In front of the whole group, ask participants to take turns stating what it is they want and who they would like to provide it. (5–10 minutes)

3. Once all the requests have been made, have a debriefing session. Participants may be feeling exposed, uncomfortable, needy, or denied. Others may have thought it a very easy exercise. Teasing out the differences in experience for each participant will help group members understand themselves more and understand more about what might get in the way of future negotiations. (10–15 minutes)

Activity 46 I Want it More

Facilitator Notes

This activity is an energizer. It can also help participants see what strategies they use to achieve their goals. *Materials:* Scarves, or several strips of strong cloth, or short rope.

1. Ask participants to pair up. Provide each pair with a scarf or a short piece of rope. (2 minutes)

2. Invite participants to start off by each holding an end of the scarf or rope and to then find a strategy that will allow them to "win" the rope. Tell them that this isn't necessarily a trial of strength. (5 minutes)

    Note: Strategies that people use in this exercise are discussion, subterfuge, seduction, tickling, sulking, and ganging up.

3. After the pairs have tried out their strategies, ask them to discuss what the strategies were and how they felt about them. Were they successful? Was there anything else they could have done? Would they have liked a different result? (5 minutes)

4. Bring the discussion back to the whole group, and share any insights. Highlight how the exercise might apply to negotiation. (5–10 minutes)

Activity 47 Getting to "Yes"

Facilitator Notes

This activity is designed to help people see how they negotiate, what strategies they adopt, how they influence others, and what happens when they have to compromise. Using money helps make the negotiations very real and often impassioned.

Briefing

1. Invite each participant to agree on a sum of money they will each place into a communal pot (say, $3 to $5). Explain that they need to be prepared to lose the money.

2. Once the sum has been agreed on and deposited into a pot or bag available for this purpose, give the group 30 to 45 minutes to make a decision about how the money is to be spent. They can each propose ideas and use all their influence to gain support or allies for their idea. The options are endless (e.g., donation to charity, buying shares, lottery tickets, treating the group to cake or champagne). Group members may even argue for the reason why it should be given to them personally. Only one idea can be chosen by the whole group by the end of the available time. The money cannot be returned to participants, because this will provide an easy way of opting out.

3. Once the decision is made, invite the group to reflect on skills. Did they give up too easily? Were they easily won over? Did they hold on tenaciously to their ideas? Were they able to compromise? How do they feel now about the decision? What methodology was used by the group to reach a decision?

4. Have another debrief once the money has been spent to check out any thoughts or feelings about the decision. (For example, if the money is gambled, some participants might be angry. If the money is invested, participants may feel freed up and energized.)

Coaching

Explore with your coachee their negotiation style. Is it about winning at all costs, or do they have a different set of principles? Do they take a "people" approach or an issues-based approach? What do they think are their strengths and weaknesses? Can they provide examples of times when they had to negotiate for something and felt they had a successful outcome? Can they think of another occasion when the outcome wasn't successful? What were the situations and what were the strategies they adopted?

Reflect on how the coachee negotiated his or her coaching contract or job contract. Was he or she assertive, passive, or aggressive? Explore his or her history of negotiation and relationship to authority.

Facilitator Self-Development

1. Acquaint yourself with Pokémon and other similar Japanese children's games, which are based on using the strengths of each team member to create success for the whole team.

2. Watch the film *Twelve Angry Men* for insights into negotiation.

3. Look up the SPIN online Web site, which teaches all about win-win strategies. Find it at www.huthwaite.co.uk.

2.10 Facilitator Support

If you are working as a facilitator with individuals or groups, there will be times when your interventions or suggestions won't work or times when you don't know or aren't sure of what action to take.

You have a responsibility to the people you are facilitating, and to yourself as a professional facilitator, to review your practice and reflect on those areas in which you may have lost perspective or become stuck. To address this issue, you will need supervision or support from other people whose experience and insight you respect. This support may vary in form, as follows:

- *Group supervision* puts you and other facilitators together with a group supervisor. This form of facilitation parallels your own team or group, and acts as a "container" for the helping relationship. It can be especially revealing to be involved with other facilitators who are also learning and reflecting on their teams or groups. Such a group will typically be challenging, supportive, and creative, generating many new ideas and options for future facilitation.

- *Formal one-to-one supervision* with a nominated supervisor who is also an experienced facilitator is another way to learn. Ideally, you will find someone who has a genuine understanding of both group process and business. However, it is in the area of process where facilitators need the most help, so don't be deterred if the individual does not have much business experience. If there is nobody within your organization who has appropriate supervision skills, look to professional bodies and schools that run groupwork training.

- *Peer coaching* is when facilitators meet with one another at regular times to support their own work and that of colleagues. The group will not have any formal leader and may look at both the ongoing issues of the group and any other issues that are affecting your performance as a facilitator. The group should always be supportive, but may well be challenging at the same time. The key issue for people who want to do this is to find ways to be open, to accept their feelings of vulnerability (the reason for being in such a group), and to avoid competitive or image-building agendas.

If you have never had supervision or are not sure what support is appropriate, here are some pointers:

1. *When do you look for support/supervision?*
   If you are working on a one-to-one basis in the workplace as a coach or mentor or are counseling staff in any respect, then you may want and need some objective points of view. It can help you see what you bring into the process, as well as what you might be leaving out.

   If you are working with groups on a regular basis as a trainer, facilitator, manager, or team leader, there will be times when others can help identify what is happening in the group, how you interpret it, what is going on between you and the group, and how you are using authority, as well as deal with difficult situations and personalities with whom you are dealing.

2. *How does such support work?*
   - An allotted time and space is set aside for this assistance. This is a priority for all participants.

- Ground rules are made between participants regarding time, space, purpose, and appropriate behaviors.

- When people want to speak, they are clear about how much time they will need. A timekeeper is nominated.

- Listeners in the group give the speaker their full attention and ask clarifying questions where appropriate.

- People are constructive and authentic with their feedback. You don't avoid telling it as you see it, but you also don't judge people for what they've done.

- People agree not to be defensive when receiving feedback.

- People's successes are celebrated.

- The group empathizes with people's difficulties.

- Any exercises or techniques offered are seen simply as one way of providing support, not the only way to do something.

3. *How do you know if it's working?*
   You will feel valued. You will feel encouraged to bring more of your problems to the group. You may come away with some good insights and ideas. You will want more of it.

Activity 48 What I Expect

Facilitator Notes

This activity is intended to help participants share personal information about themselves that they might not normally reveal and see how useful it is to share personal information and insights. This exercise can also help build trust and identity within a team or group.

Materials: A large sheet of flipchart paper for each participant.

1. Ask participants to think of one quality they bring to their work and one quality they possess but seldom reveal. Provide each participant with a sheet of flipchart paper and ask them to illustrate both qualities in whatever shape or form they wish. (10–15 minutes)

   Ask the participants to notice what feelings, judgments, and thoughts they have about their illustrations as they undertake the exercise, as well as after they have finished the task.

2. Ask participants to work in small groups, with individual participants presenting their qualities to their group. They should say something about

   - the feelings and judgments they have about their own illustration;
   - the standards they expect of themselves;
   - the standards they expect of others;
   - what will happen if those standards are not met. (15 minutes)

3. Ask other members of the team or group to listen and then give feedback. Some of the themes people might want to focus on are

   - whether or not the judgments the participant makes are reasonable;
   - whether or not they think the standards are reasonable;
   - the quality of work that they have seen the individual produce. (5–10 minutes)

4. Draw the group back together and discuss the judgments we make about ourselves, our work, and the contributions of others with whom we have to work. If we judge and drive ourselves too harshly, can we ever accept support from others? And would we be able to truly support others? (10–15 minutes)

Activity 49 Risk and Failure

Facilitator Notes

This activity will help people explore how they feel about failure. In an organizational setting, this might be an unusual topic, because people are generally not encouraged to admit their mistakes. However, when it comes to learning, we know that it is often through our mistakes that we gain our most valuable insights. Furthermore, if we share our own, we can help others avoid making the same mistakes.

1. Ask participants to consider a mistake (either large or small) that they have seen other people make and what the repercussions of that mistake were. If they can't think of anything, ask them to consider great sporting or political gaffes. Ask them to write down:

   • what the mistake was;
   • what they felt about it;
   • what its repercussions were;
   • what happened afterward;
   • whether or not the individual "recovered" with minimal damage to business, reputation, public approval, and so on. (5–10 minutes)

2. Now ask participants to consider what would constitute a "significant" failure in their own working life. Ask participants to consider realistic examples and to write down

   • what the failure would be;
   • what they would expect the reaction to be;
   • how they would manage such an event;
   • whether or not they would expect to recover from such failure. (5–10 minutes)

3. Ask participants to form pairs or groups of three, and to share their examples and their written responses. (5 minutes per person, followed by a 5-minute discussion among the groups regarding their similarities and differences)

4. Draw the group back together and ask participants to place their personal tolerance of failure on a continuum in the room. Tell participants that there is an imaginary line running across the room that represents failure as a learning experience at one end and failure as a weakness at the other. People should place themselves along this continuum, depending on where they see themselves. You, as facilitator, ask various participants, as they stand in their positions, why they have placed themselves there, what views they hold in that position, and whether or not after they have spoken, they want to change position. (10–15 minutes)

◄—The Continuum—►

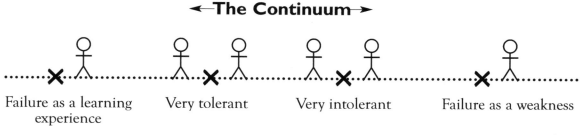

Failure as a learning experience   Very tolerant   Very intolerant   Failure as a weakness

(continued)

Activity 49 Risk and Failure *(concluded)*

5. Draw the group back together and facilitate a discussion on failure. What can people learn from failure? What tolerance levels do we have for failure? What does this mean in terms of gaining support? (10–15 minutes)

Note: Success is a polar opposite to failure. Bring into the discussion the notion of success and how that is treated in companies. What recognition is there when someone succeeds? What support do people get when they are successful?

Coaching

As a manager, you are in an excellent position to support someone who is facilitating other groups or teams at work. One of the first things you must do is determine how much support the coachee needs. How pressing are the issues they are facing? How much time do they need? If you feel that you can provide the support required, allocate a set time (say one hour), and use your coaching skills to support, empathize, and give your full attention to the process.

A simple structure to follow is to ask your coachee to present a single issue or incident with which they are concerned. Ask them for details about the incident—who were the people involved, what was the context, what actually happened, and how they responded.

Remember that you are not looking to provide answers here. Rather, it is your role to prompt the coachee to find their own answers. You need to trust that they have the resources within them; otherwise, you will be creating dependence. However, you can offer models or insights that you think might be relevant to the situation, and you can certainly help your coachee review what happened and look at what alternative strategies they might have adopted. As coach, it is your role to raise the awareness and responsibility in the coachee of their part in the situation in the most helpful way possible. This may require sitting with them and pondering the situation, challenging their behavior, valuing their efforts, and encouraging them to look at what else they might be able to do. However, don't try to solve the situation for them. Although you might have a clever solution, remember that the coachee will always have to face situations on their own.

Facilitator Self-Development

1. Get some support. Make sure you've had experience with a support group, a mentor, or a coach. Feel for yourself what it is like to disclose your vulnerabilities and be challenged. Most importantly, you need to see that mistakes are useful and that they provide gateways to learning.

2. Watch the video *Conducting Business*, featuring Ben Zander (published by GNP Ltd: www.gnp.co.uk).

PART THREE
Creative Facilitation

3.1 One-to-One Facilitation

As a facilitator, there will be many times when you are called upon to work with an individual on a one-to-one basis. This might be in an appraisal, a performance review situation, a coaching scenario, or even within a team setting. You will need to know what you are trying to achieve and which interventions will best serve the person with whom you are working.

One-to-one facilitation has much in common with coaching, but it is not exactly the same. The business coach is focused on the performance of the individual, and will advise, guide, and counsel the employee to that effect. The facilitator has more responsibility. If performance focus is required, the facilitator needs to be able to work with goals and objectives. However, the skilled facilitator will also be able to move into the mentoring role of one-to-one interaction, which typically involves a more hands-off approach than coaching. There is less focus on short-term goals, and a greater emphasis on self-awareness.

Meanwhile, the facilitator may choose to work with an individual in the team or group setting so that others in the team can learn from the challenges being faced by the individual team member.

What is always most important to establish in all scenarios is the contract. As a manager, it might be clear that you have some line-management responsibilities. As a coach or mentor, there may well be a three-way contract involving you, the participant, and the sponsor (for example, the participant's manager). When working one-to-one within a team, you will typically get agreement from the individual participant to work with them "in the moment," for their benefit as well as for the benefit of the wider team (who will learn by observation).

You need to both be clear how far and to what depth you are going to work, the ways in which you will work, how long the work will last, and what outcomes you and the participant expect from your one-to-one interventions. This contract will ensure that the fundamentals of safety, openness, and trust are maintained.

So how do you work most effectively on a one-to-one basis?

Clearly you will need to build your theoretical understanding and your practical skills. One of the most useful models for facilitators is that of the experiential learning cycle (on the right).

This starts with the experiences of the individual (for example, their difficulties with a particular customer or client). The facilitator will help them think about their experience in more detail. What was their part in it? What skills did they use? Who else was involved?

The facilitator will then help the participant make sense of what happened. Their work at this stage of the cycle might be to provide models, to discuss the experiences of others and to highlight other influences that might have been in play. With their new comprehension of the situation, the participant can then take appropriate action. This may be planning what to do for next time, building new skills, or trying a new approach.

The simple experiential-learning model builds awareness in the participant about their part in the situation and helps them take responsibility for what to do next. Furthermore, it can be adapted to the needs of the situation you are facing.

Finally, a word about your approach. When you are facilitating one-to-one, you will need to pay special attention to valuing (see Section 1.7). This provides the basis of your relationship. Make sure you have good listening and observation skills, and make sure you know what you are trying to achieve. Working with someone else, in depth, can be one of the richest forms of facilitation and can lead to real and lasting change.

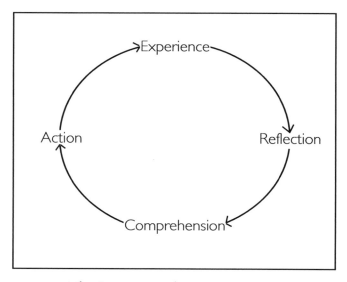

The Experiential Learning Cycle

Activity 50 One-to-One Skills Building

Facilitator Notes

Here is a range of short one-to-one exercises that you can use with your team or with trainee facilitators to help build up their skills in four critical areas:

- *Observation.* Ask participants to pair up and to talk to each other for 5 minutes about one of the following topics: their next deadline, their worst customer, their usual trip to work. (5 minutes)

    After they have spoken, ask participants to sit back-to-back and, without turning around, to say what their partner is wearing, what color their eyes are, and what nonverbal cues they picked up. (5 minutes)

    Then facilitate a discussion about observation and how important it is in giving people one-to-one attention. Discuss whether participants found it easy or difficult. (5–10 minutes)

- *Listening and reflecting back.* In pairs, ask participants to take turns talking for 5 minutes about the issue of work and life balance. (5 minutes per participant)

    It is the listeners' task to demonstrate interest (for example, with nods and eye contact) and continue to listen, even when their partner says something they disagree with. They should notice any internal chatter that goes on and, at appropriate times, reflect back key words or phrases that they have heard. At the end of the 5 minutes, the speakers and listeners should rate on a scale of 1 to 10 how positive the listening was and whether or not there were any distractions.

- *Summarizing.* Ask participants to pair up and discuss for 5 minutes any significant one-to-one work they have undertaken. If they haven't undertaken any, ask them to explore what they think might be involved, and what they might get out of it. Their partner in the exercise summarizes in a few words or sentences, no more than once or twice during the 5 minutes, the key points that they have heard. (5 minutes per participant, plus feedback)

- *Questioning.* Ask participants to pair up and speak in turn about the importance of building relationships at work. It is the listener's task to see if they can deepen the process by asking one or two open questions (who, what, where, when, how) that challenge and encourage the speaker to be more specific and raise awareness.

    Note: Be careful of "why" questions (these can evoke defensive reactions) and leading questions (which are easily spotted and can feel manipulative). (5 minutes per participant, plus feedback)

Activity 51 Hands-on Coaching

Facilitator Notes

This creative exercise can be used to open up a discussion on who leads and who follows in one-to-one facilitation. The answer to this question is that facilitators need to be flexible in their response and empowering in their approach.

1. Ask participants to pair up. Participant A should place their right hand out in front of them, palm down. Participant B places their left hand, palm down, on top of A's hand so that there is distinct but minimal contact. Participant B then closes their eyes.

2. Participant A then moves their hand, slowly. It is Participant B's task to follow any movement A makes without opening their eyes. It is A's task to build up trust with their partner—not to make any sudden movements, but to build up confidence so that B follows freely. (2–3 minutes per participant).

    Note: For those participants who find the exercise simple, an advanced instruction is for the pairs to use both their hands (but still keep their eyes closed).

3. Facilitate a discussion. What has this activity got to do with coaching? (trust, leadership, awareness) Were there times when it was no longer clear who was leading and who was following? (5–10 minutes)

Activity 52 In-Depth One-to-One Practice

Facilitator Notes

This is an in-depth exercise that helps people see what development they might need in order to build up their own one-to-one skills. It will also give them experience in facilitating others.

1. Ask people to work in groups of three. Instruct them to facilitate a 30-minute one-to-one session that focuses on development needs. Participant A acts as coachee, Participant B as the coach, and Participant C as the observer.

2. Participant A responds to questions and prompts from the coach. It is his or her task to be as authentic as possible and to discuss real one-to-one self-development issues.

3. Participant B's tasks are
   - to establish the contract (length of time, way of working, focus);
   - to practice one-to-one skills (listening, questioning, observing, summarizing);
   - to manage the time;
   - to elicit A's one-to-one strengths (e.g., experience, skills, qualities), challenges (e.g., people, company culture, time constraints), and opportunities (e.g., performance-management scenarios, formal coaching schemes, team situations).

(continued)

Activity 52 In-Depth One-to-One Practice (concluded)

4. Participant C's tasks are

   - to observe and be ready to provide constructive feedback on B's one-to-one coaching style, the skills used, and nonverbal communication;
   - to look for what is left unsaid or things that A or B missed;
   - to observe A's and B's nonverbal communication.

5. At the end of the session, C facilitates a 5 to 10 minute feedback session, which starts with a self-assessment from B. Then A gives his or her feedback on how it was to be facilitated. Finally, C provides his or her observations and feedback. (10–15 minutes)

6. When everyone has played all three roles, draw the whole group back together and highlight what skills people already have, what skills they need to develop, what opportunities exist for one-to-one work, and what further support or training they need. (15–20 minutes)

Facilitator Self-Development

The following suggestions can help you explore one-to-one facilitation:

1. Make sure you have some personal experience. If you haven't been coached, counseled, or mentored, look for company projects or programs you can become involved with or commit to some professional development in which there is a significant emphasis on one-to-one work.

2. Build your theoretical knowledge by reading journal articles or visiting Web sites on the subject.

3. Practice listening, paraphrasing, and reflecting back. When someone is talking to you face-to-face or on the phone, take the opportunity to understand what is really being asked and to build your one-to-one skills. Where possible, make sure you are in a place where you won't be interrupted. Give full attention and check your understanding.

4. Use a learning journal in which you record your thoughts, feelings, insights, and experiences. A learning journal acts rather like a personal mentor and helps you build your self-awareness. Find one that you can carry around with you and conveniently make notes in.

3.2 Powering Up Self-Confidence

Facilitators need to have an idea of the impact they make on individuals and groups through their personal "presence."

Presence is drawn from the combination of your own personality, energy, enthusiasm, and magnetism. It is a set of qualities that needs careful attention and honing, and requires continuous personal development. If you have a passion for your subject or for people, it is through your presence that you can enhance your authority and build confidence in your work.

Charismatic facilitators or speakers talk with passion and credibility because they have worked out what their values and beliefs are. As a result, they capture attention. Think for a moment about politicians; love or hate them, the ones who are most commanding are not necessarily the ones who speak the most sense, but the ones who inspire with their conviction.

Everyone is born with natural presence, but as we grow up and fit in with the demands of society, we tend to lose our presence. It is often the roles we play in life that influence how we behave. Take the example of a police officer whose uniform shapes their social role, behavior, even grammar.

To a certain extent, we all subjugate our natural presence to the context in which we work. The question is, how do we break out of such ingrained behavior?

Barriers to Presence

One of the traps into which facilitators fall (that takes away from their personal presence) is adopting an idealized view of what a facilitator should be. It is all very well and good to model our behavior on best practice, but if we can never live up to the standards we set for ourselves, we feel inadequate about who we are and what competencies we have. The danger comes when we get confused between what we can do naturally and what an ideal facilitator would do in a similar situation. We need to believe that we are good enough just as we are, and we must recognize that idealization only feeds self-limiting beliefs. When we get it right, it is not because we have reached the ideal; it is because we are being more fully ourselves.

Facilitators must also stop trying to avoid exposing too much of ourselves. It becomes a way of life that diminishes who we are because we are constantly trying to live up to other people's rules, moral codes, and instructions instead of having and taking responsibility for our own. Facilitators who open up become recharged and comfortable with themselves, and are more passionate about what they are doing because their vision and commitment underpins what they set out to achieve.

Embracing Success

Ways to power up your presence:

- Consciously choose to go as far as you can with all that you have.

- Build awareness of your strengths and weaknesses. Discover what it is that you have to learn, and build on those qualities.

- Make sure that you know what your values are in your personal and professional life. Test them out with others, be prepared to stand by them, and find out what happens when people challenge you on them. Your values are the bedrock of who you are. Let them inform your vision, your goals, and your intention.

- Be physically present. Become more aware of how you walk, stand, sit, move, and gesture. If necessary, get some coaching on improving breathing and posture.

- Work on your attentiveness—your listening, your observing, and your intuition (use your hunches to guide you).

- Work on the way you speak—the way you convey meaning—as well as the modulations of tone and voice. Discover the power of nonverbal communication.

Activity 53 Trying "Not to Lose"

Facilitator Notes

This exercise is designed to help facilitators and managers think about how much time they spend trying "not to lose," instead of enjoying success.

1. Draw the following diagram on flipchart paper. Using the theory, describe briefly to the group what you mean by trying "not to lose" and "embracing and enjoying success." (5–10 minutes)

Embracing Success	*Trying "not to lose"*
Positive values	Defensive strategies
Physical presence	No risks
Attentiveness	Other people's rules
Being fully who you are	Being less than you are

2. Split the team or group into two small groups, and give each group one of the following passages (see below). Invite the groups to come up with a short playlet (everyone should have a role) that reflects the speaker's meaning and that demonstrates the physical characteristics of each concept. Encourage them to be creative, and remind them that this is an opportunity to practice presence. (Give the groups 20 minutes to discuss and prepare their playlet.)

Embracing success: *Our deepest fear is not that we are inadequate. Our deepest fear is that we are powerful beyond measure. It is our light—not our darkness—that most frightens us. We ask ourselves,* Who am I to be brilliant, gorgeous, talented, fabulous? *Actually, who are you not to be? . . . Your playing small doesn't serve the world. There's nothing enlightened about shrinking so that other people won't feel insecure around you. We are all meant to shine, as children do. We were born to manifest the glory that is within us. It's not just in some of us. It's in everyone. And as we let our own light shine, we unconsciously give other people permission to do the same. As we're liberated from our own fear, our presence automatically liberates others.* (Taken from Nelson Mandela's *Long Walk to Freedom*).

Trying "not to lose": Shortly after Karl Wallenda fell to his death in 1978 traversing a 75-ft. high wire in downtown San Juan, Puerto Rico, his wife, also an aerialist, discussed that fateful San Juan walk: *"Perhaps his most dangerous,"* she recalled. *"All Karl thought about for three straight months prior to it was falling. It was the first time he'd ever thought about that, and it seemed too that he put all his energies into not falling rather than walking the tightrope."* Mrs. Wallenda added that her husband even went so far as to personally supervise the installation of the tightrope, making certain that the guy wires were secure, *"Something he had never even thought of doing before."*

(continued)

Activity 53 Trying "Not to Lose" (concluded)

From what we learned from the interviews with successful leaders, it became increasingly clear that when Karl Wallenda poured his energies into not falling rather than walking the tightrope, he was virtually destined to fall. (Taken from Warren Bennis and Burt Nanus, *Leaders–the Strategies for Taking Charge*).

3. They should then enact the playlet for the whole group. (5 minutes per group)

4. Facilitate a discussion on what participants experienced in the playlet and then invite participants to talk about the times when people try "not to lose" and the times when they embrace success. What strategies do they tend to adopt now? Are there any obvious strategies that they could adopt that would help them change? (10–15 minutes)

Activity 54 Hot Seat

Facilitator Notes

When you want to empower people by helping them raise their level of self-confidence and present their best self, one of the most direct and powerful ways to do that is through group coaching. It provides that rare opportunity for people to talk about themselves to a group whose only task is to be attentive.

1. Invite individual group or team members to take turns occupying "the hot seat" for 5 minutes (simply a chair at the front of the room). The task for the volunteer is simply to talk about him- or herself in an authentic and fully present way. (5 minutes)

2. The rest of the group watches without interruption, but observes anything they notice that detracts from the way the individual presents him- or herself (distracting twitches, finger drumming, umms and ahhs in sentences, slouched posture, inaudible voice).

3. After the 5 minutes are up, ask the participant in the hot seat to give a self-assessment and then ask for the feedback from the group. Ask someone in the group to take notes so that they can remember both the positives as well as those things that the participant might want to develop. (5–10 minutes)

4. If there is a particular aspect of the participant's "presentation" that could do with some immediate improvement, such as posture or breathing, invite the occupier of the hot seat to take another turn to practice these aspects. Alternatively, after everyone has had a turn in the hot seat, ask the group to get into pairs and repeat the process, receiving intensive coaching and support from their partner. (10 minutes each way).

Note: In this activity, some people may feel self-conscious or feel that they have nothing to say. As the facilitator, gently encourage them, because they will be meeting the blocks that get in the way of their own self-confidence. If they get really stuck, you can prompt by asking them to describe what it is they do at work, and what qualities they bring to the team.

Activity 55 Body Talk

Facilitator Notes

This creative activity helps people understand the things that get in the way of personal presence. It is an exercise that also helps people identify what is distinctive in their own facilitator style.

1. In small groups, each participant takes 5 minutes to tell a story or anecdote to the rest of the group. The group is to pay attention to personal style and identify any "blocks" to presence. The group then provides feedback on what went well and what might need more attention.

    Feedback guidelines. Is the speaker blocking themselves in any of these areas?

    *   *Posture.* What is working against them? Where are their tensions? Where is their energy?
    *   *Breathing.* Is their breathing too shallow? Does it change? Do they use their breath positively (e.g., for dramatic effect)?
    *   *Pacing.* How do they pace their talk? Do they need to speed up? Or slow down? Do they use pauses or silences? Do they give the audience time to reflect?
    *   *Inflection.* How do they end? Ending on an "up" can mean self-doubt or create expectations. Inflection "down" conveys a real belief in what you are saying. It lends gravitas and weight to your words.
    *   *Tone.* Do they sound authentic? Or are unintended messages coming through, such as sarcasm or anger?
    *   *Hands.* What are they saying with their hands? Do they use them to energize the group? Do their hand movements reinforce the message? Or detract from it?
    *   *Eyes.* Is their contact engaging, distant, or staring? Do they provide a holding focus?
    *   *Voice.* Are they suffering from performance anxiety? How would you describe their voice?

Coaching

You will undoubtedly have some intuitive sense of your coachee's strengths and weaknesses regarding presence after working with them for a few weeks. Talk to them about how they come across to others and how they can power up their presence by exploring areas that impede it. Use the Body Talk activity (Activity 55), and work with the coachee to explore and analyze the qualities, behaviors, and body language of someone he or she knows who has charisma and powerful presence. Invite the coachee to analyze him- or herself in the same way and to take an inventory of those qualities and behaviors that add to his or her charisma as well as those that detract from presence. Some areas you might want to encourage the coachee to investigate: making new relationships, maintaining relationships, and the impressions that other people have of him or her. Encourage the coachee to elicit some feedback from people he or she works with and trusts.

Another avenue to explore with the coachee is values. How does the coachee convey these values in his or her work and the relationships he or she has with others? Once people are standing firmly in their values, they immediately have more presence.

Finally, make sure that the coachee has identified specific ways to power up his or her presence, and see that he or she takes suitable steps to practice and develop those skills, behaviors, and characteristics. Set targets and encourage them to evaluate their progress regularly.

Facilitator Self-Development

1. The blocks we experience in being present usually involve a rule of some kind that was imposed in the past. Presence fully abounds in small children, and then life tends to squash the delight through rules about behavior, noise levels, and so on. These rules then become blocks to presence. (If there were no blocks, presence would not be a problem.) Discover your blocks and other people blocks by paying attention to some of the following clues:

   - Uncommunicated thoughts and feelings are blocks to presence because they distract individuals from paying attention to the here and now.

   - Feelings that keep us from becoming all we can be can present themselves at any time. (For example, if you have difficulty dealing with anger, your skills may be immobilized by the fear and dread of an angry person being in the group.)

   - It is important to help yourself as much as possible: Identify your strengths and weaknesses, and find ways of working with them to strengthen your coping mechanisms.

   - Identify what makes you different, and incorporate it into your personal style and presence. Explore and accept the gifts that you have. Commit to yourself.

2. Observe politicians or actors you admire, and discover what works for them.

3. Join a community theatre, a singing class, or a poetry-reading group.

4. Join a yoga class: it will help you become more aware of movement and posture. Make sure the class includes the practice of yogic breathing (pranayama).

3.3 Facilitating without Words

As a facilitator, you must be sensitive to what people are *not* saying, understand the power of silence, and pick up on the nonverbal signals that people give off. This is what facilitating without words is all about. Mastery of this important set of skills can add immeasurably to your effectiveness and presence.

Body Signals

Let's say you are working as a facilitator in a meeting and you need to help the team come to a decision. By reading body signals, you can see who is sitting back, who is banging the table, and who is sitting on the fence. These everyday terms have a physical expression. People who are sitting back will often be leaning back in their chairs with their arms folded, or sitting on their hands. Fence sitters will often be fidgeting in their chairs as they are persuaded first by one argument and then by the other—they look as uncomfortable as they are.

By noticing these signals, you gain insight into the unspoken attitudes of the team and team members, and can use this information to intervene and break the pattern. ("I see you're sitting back, John; I wonder if you have views that you haven't shared yet.") This sort of intervention can bring people into the meeting who might be important to the decision-making process; by focusing on their physical characteristics, you are highlighting where their energy might be stuck.

Another signal that you will undoubtedly pick up on as a facilitator is the tendency of some people to direct questions or comments to you during a debate or discussion. Imagine, however, that you are trying to empower the team, rather than leading it authoritatively. How can you respond to these unspoken requests for leadership? The trick here is to notice the gaze of the person as they leave their question or demand hanging in the air and "pass it on" by deliberately looking to the person next to you as if they might have an answer. By passing on the look, you are communicating nonverbally to the team that you are not always going to provide answers to their questions—that this is an area where they are able to take responsibility for their own solutions.

Attentive Silence, and What Isn't Being Said

Another important aspect of facilitating without words is to be comfortable with silence (see Activity 58).

In today's world, work and silence seem like polar opposites. After all, there is so much communication at work—so many phones, so many meetings, so much busyness. Perhaps it is because of this frenetic activity that attentive silence has so much power. It slows down the usual pace of the task, and helps people see what is getting in the way of the objective.

Whether you are working with a team or group or on a one-to-one basis, you need to be able to sit with silence. This doesn't mean closing your eyes and drifting away. On the contrary, it is about watching and observing and waiting with expectant attention.

Silence will quietly but effectively put the pressure on people to say what is going on in the here and now. Your ability to wait for them to say what is happening encourages them to say what often remains unsaid.

Within every team or group, there are things that aren't spoken about. Take the example of gender differences: although this might be a real issue of concern in some teams and groups, unless it is brought up as a specific topic within, say, an equal-opportunities context, it is typically not discussed openly. Yet you can bet that within any mixed-sex team, there will be unspoken thoughts and feelings about who gets on best with whom, and why.

Sometimes you will need to challenge the unspoken culture of the team (see Activity 57). Be sure you do not punish people for what they don't say; instead, encourage people to reflect on how the team is working together. You can probably expect a stormy or passionate debate, so beware: people stay quiet for good reasons. But if you are looking to serve the team, it can be helpful to focus on what is not said. In my experience, once these issues are out in the open, they lose much of their dramatic charge.

Activity 56 Beyond Words

Facilitator Notes

This activity helps people understand how our body reflects our mental or emotional tension. "Stiff-necked," "square-jawed," "tight-lipped" people are stereotypes, but the terms represent insight into people we have to meet and do business with. Facilitators need to be able to pick up these clues. This activity helps people see exactly what signals they and others unconsciously send out.

1. Introduce the concept of nonverbal communication (see theory) and how nonverbal signals can be read consciously by facilitators. (10–15 minutes)

2. Invite two volunteers from the team or group to stand up at the front of the room and ask all the observers to notice and compare the different body characteristics that they see in the people they are looking at. (The reason you need to have two people stand at the same time is because there will always be differences that are apparent between two people. It is therefore easier for the observers, and less intrusive for the volunteers.)

   However, tell participants to limit themselves only to descriptions of what they see. They must not interpret. ("I see that Robert balances his weight mainly on one leg, while Jane shifts from one side to the other" is fine, but "I see that Robert balances his weight mainly on one side, and I suspect he's always off-balance" is not OK.) (5 minutes)

3. Ask the pair of volunteers to turn around so that they are facing away from the team or group. Again, invite descriptions and comparisons of body characteristics. (5 minutes)

4. Once everyone has completed their observation, invite each participant to come up with a word or quality that they think best represents the "body reading" of the volunteers (e.g., "solid," "energetic," "pent-up"). At this stage, don't ask for a response from the volunteers; just see if they can stay with what they have heard until the end of the session. (5 minutes)

5. Ask the next pair of volunteers to present themselves for a body reading, and repeat the procedure until everyone has been "read." (5 minutes)

6. Facilitate a general discussion about the exercise. Did people struggle, or did they find that once they started to look, it was easier than they thought? Did it get easier as they went along? Did people feel it was accurate? Or was it a stab in the dark? Did they trust their assessments? For those who were being "read," did the observations feel accurate? Were they surprised by what people saw in them? How would they use this technique in the real world? (10–15 minutes)

Activity 57 Under the Carpet

Facilitator Notes

Certain subjects in some groups are not discussed by a kind of unspoken agreement. This is normal, but if you are a facilitator working with an established team and you feel as though people are withholding or that things aren't being said that should be said, free it up with this simple activity.

1. Draw a line across the middle of a piece of flipchart paper. Brainstorm with the team on those topics or subjects that are acceptable to talk about (above the carpet) and those that are not (under the carpet). (5–10 minutes)

2. Identify with the team any "under the carpet" issues that are holding back learning or progress. Facilitate a team discussion about how important issues that need to be addressed can be included in a more conscious and open way. (10–15 minutes)

Activity 58 Waiting for Godot

Facilitator Notes

Another important technique for facilitators is to be comfortable with silence. This is especially important in teams or groups where "process" is uncomfortable (yet extremely revealing). By deliberately allowing silence and giving people time to stay with what is going on at deeper unspoken levels, the facilitator can help whatever is going on within the team to emerge.

1. Ask participants to be on their own for 15 minutes to experience complete silence. If possible, allow participants to wander outside. If this is difficult, provide a collection of objects (stones, shells, toys, evocative objects) and postcards (with a variety of people and scenes) for participants to choose and contemplate.

   During this time, instruct the participants to find something not related to work (or to choose one of the items provided) that completely absorbs their attention. They should not try to describe it or analyze it (and certainly not talk about it). Rather, they should see if they can absorb it, see it in as much detail as possible, and meditate on it. Ask them only to experience:
   - the connection between themselves and whatever it is they are observing, as a monk would do when meditating about a stone; and
   - the nature of the silence they are experiencing. (15 minutes)

2. Ask participants to pair up and take turns talking about their 15-minute experience. Put these themes on a flipchart for prompts:
   - Would you have liked more time for this exercise?
   - What did the quality of your silence feel like?
   - What was the quality of your attention like?
   - What judgments did you make about yourself, the activity, and the object of your attention?

(continued)

Activity 58 Waiting for Godot (*concluded*)

3. It is the partner-facilitator's task to stay with what their partner-speaker is saying and to empathize nonverbally (that is, by showing attention). They must not jump in if a silence develops. See what emerges from the silence, and allow the partner to deepen their experience. After 10 minutes, the second participant in the pair—the facilitator—should summarize the main points of what they have heard and reflect them back to their partner. (10 minutes)

4. Switch roles. (10 minutes)

5. Ask a volunteer to facilitate a discussion with the group on silence. What were participants' experiences? Were there any insights? Do people feel that there are any cultural obstacles to periods of silence? Stress that it is the facilitator's task to model best practice. If nobody has any comments about the subject, the facilitator should allow the silence to happen and wait patiently to see what might emerge. (15 minutes)

6. If time allows, encourage the team to give feedback to the practice facilitator. How well were they able to follow the process of the team or group discussion? Did they have the opportunity to facilitate silence? Were they able to encourage reflection within the group?

   Give time for the facilitator to assess their own experience. Did what they experienced match the feedback received? (10–15 minutes)

Coaching

The "Rule of 3" is a useful model for coaches and coachees when a team or group is stuck and frustrated and where the facilitator or a team member is feeling welling anger or hostility: The Rule of 3 can help you by identifying whether or not the feelings are

- yours (you are angry about the situation and/or something in your past has been triggered by the current situation);

- someone else's (somebody else is angry or feeling hostile, but is not expressing it clearly and you are picking up their unexpressed emotions); or

- the group's (this is a group issue that doesn't belong to any one individual, but rather to the collective whole).

Models in coaching are useful, as they provide the hooks on which your coachees can "hang" their own experience. Models should not be proffered as the "truth," but rather as potentially helpful ways in which the coachee can gain insight and stay focused when working with others.

Facilitator Self-Development

Don't get tripped up by your own nonverbal communication. Observe others closely and work on how you deal with things that aren't said.

1. Get someone to body-read you. Ask them to identify in a single word or phrase what your normal body language says to them.

2. Reflect on the body expression and metaphorical truth of the following statements:

   Two-faced—pain in the neck—sinking your teeth into—lily-livered—no backbone—shouldering a burden—pissed off—thick-skinned—starry-eyed—tight-fisted—yellow-bellied—nose out of joint—hair-raising—skin of your teeth—itching to do it—cheeky—sniffy—heavy-handed—open-armed

3. Reflect on the following Rumi poem:

   > Silence is the sea and speech is like a river
   > The sea is seeking you: don't seek the river
   > Don't turn your head away
   > from the signs offered by the sea.

3.4 Defense Patterns

Defense mechanisms are sophisticated human responses to threats that individuals use to control life and render it safe for them. In groups, these protective mechanisms abound, and one of the difficulties for facilitators is that we never quite know which issue will trigger which defenses for each person.

You need to be aware of what some of the defense patterns are and what may lie behind them. This will give you some indication of what is going on. Here are some defensive patterns in groups:

1. *Fight patterns* are clearly at play when you have group members competing with you, being cynical about the group or topic, or indulging in aggressive questioning (which typically acts as a blocking mechanism).

2. *Flight patterns* can be seen in nervous humor, excessive gossip, withdrawal from participation in the group, rationalization, and intellectualization (which helps individuals stay away from their feelings by talking about them instead of expressing them). Flight patterns are also at play in *projection*, where people react to traits in others without recognizing that they have some of those same traits too (for example, complaining that someone is taking up too much time, when what you really want is for the group to listen to *you*).

3. *Group flighting* is behavior that lets you know that group members are protecting themselves from deeper involvement. It can be seen in the following behaviors:

   • *pairings*: small subgroups protect and look out for one another

   • *rescuing*: group members jump in to defend one another in the face of challenge in a bid to keep things safe

   • *spotlighting*: whole groups "spotlight" one member in order to deflect attention from themselves

   • *collusion*: group members all support one another in order to avoid issues that are difficult

   • *scapegoating*: one person is blamed for the difficulties a group is experiencing, instead of each member looking at their own role in the problem

Remember that these defenses (and we each have our favorites) are employed at times when people feel threatened or stressed, for whatever reason. Defenses sustain us when times are hard and give us a sense of security and self-esteem (even if they are also self-limiting). In the face of an experience that seems overwhelming, they also become a way of shoring up our own power. Because of this, facilitators have to be very wary of trampling over people's defense mechanisms. It is important to trust that they are there for a good reason and that they are a protection against past rejections, hurts, and distresses.

Consider also that when people are in groups, they often automatically adopt the role they held in their own family. For example, eldest children tend to readily take on responsibility in a group, while younger children often expect more guidance from other group members. Obviously, this is not the absolute truth, but it is a phenomenon that can help you make sense of group behavior.

As a facilitator, think about the role you took in your family. You are not exempt from group dynamics (indeed, you are right at the center of them), so you need to know how your own past experience serves or hinders you as a facilitator.

The general message here is that you should tread carefully when it comes to people's defense patterns and see what they can tell you. Develop a range of interventions that enable you to gently challenge the behavior of people in the group without reinforcing their defensive patterns. If someone already feels defensive and is then criticized, they will retreat even further from you and the group. But if that person can be accepted, recognized for what they can bring to the group, and treated in an adult way, then they can feel heartened and encouraged to participate. Try not to put group members on the spot by highlighting an element of their behavior, or they will feel victimized. Instead, make observations and interventions to the whole group. If a group is particularly cynical, invite the cynicism into the room and give it voice so that it does not lurk in the shadows and undermine the task.

As ever, stay objective. People will get provoked and defensive in the groups you run. That is the nature of groups. It is your task not to get drawn in.

Activity 59 On the Defensive

Facilitator Notes

Use this activity when you want to demonstrate the need to stand firm and not get drawn in when people's defenses are triggered. Make sure that you have read and understood the basic theory.

1. Explain to the group that when people's defenses are triggered, they will try to get you, the facilitator, involved in their drama. This presents a challenge for facilitators: to be able to spot defensiveness and work with individuals or the whole group in appropriate ways. (5–10 minutes)

2. Ask for a volunteer to facilitate a role-play on defense patterns. Explain to the whole group that this is a role-play in which the whole group will be involved. The topic on which the facilitator will be asked to run a session is "trust." How much trust do people need of one another? What does it mean to be open? How much trust actually exists in the group? (See activities on valuing and openness, if you need some ideas for possible related exercises.)

   If the volunteer facilitator needs support, allow him or her to choose a coach from the group with whom to work out a strategy beforehand. If things get out of hand during the role-play, they can also ask the group to "freeze" or stop all conversation so that the facilitator can discuss with his or her coach what has happened and what should be done next. This technique of slowing down the process and talking about what is happening and what to do next is very useful for learning. It gives the facilitator a measure of control and allows the whole group to see what sort of choices can be made.

   Explain to the volunteer facilitator that he or she is likely to have to face a difficult group where people are defensive, and that the main task is to make sure that he or she doesn't lose ground. Explain that he or she should mirror back fight patterns without getting defensive, and try to highlight flight patterns without spotlighting people too much. The volunteer facilitator should highlight to the whole group what he or she sees happening if people go into group fighting behavior. (preparation time 10 minutes)

3. Invite one or two group members to each choose one of the following roles. Participants should take the roles seriously and be realistic, but they should also try to demonstrate the characteristics of their role:

   - *Fight patterns:* You are to be competitive, cynical, or belligerent. Ask aggressive questions, cast doubt on the exercise, and cast doubt on the facilitator. Alternatively, compete with the facilitator by suggesting your own better interpretations of people's behavior. Your main task is to confront the facilitator, but be open to the facilitator's interventions if they are appropriate.

   - *Flight patterns:* You are to indulge in fooling around, withdrawal, or intellectualization about your feelings. Try not to engage in any process, although you should be willing to respond to the facilitator if you think that the facilitator's interventions are appropriate and are likely to succeed.

   - *Group flighting:* You have a choice here. You can pair up and protect each other, OR you can try to scapegoat someone in the group who you think is most to blame for the situation you are in, OR you can try to rescue each other if the going gets rough. Again, if the facilitator's interventions are authentic, you should be ready to respond genuinely.

(continued)

Activity 59 On the Defensive (*concluded*)

4. Allow the role-play to run for 10 to 15 minutes.

5. After the role-play, debrief the group (feelings may be running high). Make sure the facilitator gets some constructive feedback from the group, and explore with the group any other strategies that might have worked on the various defense patterns that were role-played. If time allows and it is appropriate, set up the exercise again with a different facilitator. (10–15 minutes)

Activity 60 It Ain't Easy

Facilitator Notes

Introduce this exercise with a team or a group of trainee facilitators to point out how people's defense strategies come into play when they are discussing sensitive issues in team or group situations. You will need a prize (such as chocolate).

1. Write the following messages on a flipchart:

women have it easy at work	*men have it easy at work*
treated with kid gloves	higher salaries
fewer expectations	it's a man's world
natural networkers	easier promotion
men have it hard at work	*women have it hard at work*
work long hours	home/career balance issues
no support	glass ceiling
a dog-eat-dog world	it's a man's world

2. Invite small groups or pairs to form and have each group discuss one of the quadrants of the above chart. Ask each group to extend the list of examples given above and be prepared to represent the view of that quadrant as forcibly as possible. Tell them that the observers/facilitator will evaluate which of the pairs/groups gives the most convincing perspective and that there will be a prize. (preparation time 10 minutes)

3. Ask one or two participants to sit out and observe group behavior, strategies in getting their points across, the impact they have on others, and what response they get. They should also evaluate which group presented the most convincing view.

4. Set a time limit of 20 minutes, and invite the groups or pairs to argue their case in the whole group. Let the discussion evolve naturally. Tell the group that it's up to them to get their view across in as persuasive a way as possible. As facilitator, your role is to contain the group, keep time, and observe. Let people

(*continued*)

have the opportunity to vent their opinions, as this is typically an issue that arouses people's feelings. Make sure you observe all the defensive dynamics that go on (fight, flight, and flighting group behavior). (20 minutes)

5. At the end of 20 minutes, call a halt and invite the group as a whole to reflect for a moment on what happened and what they noticed. Write on the flipchart any strategies they noticed themselves or others adopting. Then invite the observer(s) to feed back what they saw and who they thought was most persuasive (and how). Add in any of your own observations. Ask the observer(s) if they felt drawn into the discussion. Could they be neutral? Ask them to give the prizes to the most persuasive group—even if they didn't agree with their point of view.

    Note: The key lesson here is that we all have strategies. Some are less helpful to the group than others; but no one is immune. The skill for the facilitator is to be able to recognize the patterns, challenge them appropriately, and not get drawn in. (15 minutes)

Coaching

It is useful to work out with the coachee what his or her defense patterns are. Depending on how self-aware the coachee is, this could prove to be an easy task or a difficult task. One way to understand the qualities of defense mechanisms is to use metaphor.

Ask the coachee to imagine him- or herself as an animal. Which animal would it be? Ask the coachee to fully describe the qualities of the animal chosen. For example, a hedgehog, which is very prickly and can hurt people easily, curls up in a ball when attacked so that all their softness is protected. Then ask the coachee to describe how he or she is like the animal chosen and which of the defensive qualities described would apply to him or her.

This exercise should give you and the coachee an insight into the defenses members employ and whether or not they are flight or fight ones. Once you raise awareness of defense patterns, work can begin on finding ways of being less defensive. There may need to be some analysis of the kind of situations or people that trigger the defenses.

Once this topic has been fully explored, ask the coachee to describe fellow team members or colleagues in terms of animals, particularly those that trigger their defenses, to help the coachee understand what happens in the interactions between colleagues. Using imagery in this way can help the coachee reframe the level of power that other people have. (For instance, imagining somebody who is very prickly to be a hedgehog could help prevent the coachee from being pushed into a defensive position.)

Facilitator Self-Development

1. Facilitators have their own defense patterns. Evaluate your own so that you are not working with groups from a defensive or distressed place. The following exercise may help you identify the times or situations that trigger your defenses and provide you with alternative strategies. It is easy to fall into a defensive pattern; the skill is in recognizing when you are defensive and knowing how to break it.

    *   Think back to a time when you, as a facilitator, felt very defensive in a group. You will recognize the time, because it will be when you wanted to punish a group member or withdraw from the group. Use the theory to help you identify the kinds of behavior you displayed.

    *   Describe or write down the specific experience, behaviors, and feelings that you were having at the time.

    *   Give yourself feedback on what exactly was going on for you, the defenses you were experiencing, what triggered them, and whether or not they have any resonance with the past. For example, do you get into this particular defense pattern regularly? Or only when you are facilitating people who are more senior than you and who have particular characteristics?

    *   Think of ways you could prevent yourself from being triggered into defense patterns. Think of ways you can stay open-hearted to all group members: develop a mantra that reminds you not to take behavior personally, or remember that whatever is happening is part of the group dynamic (and something to be observed with curiosity and interest).

    *   Have contingency plans for how to get yourself out of negativity, and be ready to use interventions with the group.

3.5 Consultancy Skills

This section looks at some of the consultancy skills used in facilitation. As a facilitator, you have an expertise that is invaluable to organizations. You hold the big picture of the company and have a unique insight into the culture from working at various levels as a change agent.

In this cross-functional role, you will also have worked with people from different cultures and can provide insight into common issues and particular difficulties. The challenge is how to empower yourself and use your knowledge and wisdom in the service of the individual/team/group. How can you make observations about what you notice in the work culture without being perceived as attacking, defensive, or rude? As with many of these skills, applying them is far more difficult than talking about them.

Potency

Potency in our context refers to how we use our power to serve people positively and benignly: not shying from issues, but focusing on the big picture to help people make sense of what might be happening or what people might be feeling. As a result, your interventions will not be tied to any particular outcome and will be nonjudgmental. You have to remember that in any group you facilitate, the role you have will automatically afford you power. It is up to you to remember that it is always there and must be used fairly. Teams or groups will experience your potency when you

- use your insights to inform the group about individual and group behavior;
- state what you notice about the group process;
- use your gut reactions as a barometer of the emotional life of the group;

- make interventions so that the group can confront what it most wants to avoid; and
- use your potency to foster independence, rather than let the group push you into giving them all the answers.

Permission

Give the group "permission" to extend themselves by modeling openness, credibility, and authenticity. Set broad parameters so that there is more room for creativity, and expand horizons rather than limit them. Remember, however, that you don't want the limits to be so broad that people feel unsafe; there is a distinction between creative chaos and destructive chaos.

Encourage people to experiment, and reassure them about their own important role in the group and the intrinsic value of an exercise or discussion. You should demonstrate an understanding of the helping process within the context of a professional life.

If you shy away from valuing others or displaying your range of skills, you won't be serving the group or yourself. "Permission" is also about giving yourself encouragement to go further and dare to bring into the relationship with the group more of yourself that you might normally censor.

Protection

If groups trust you, they will let you take them almost anywhere, so you will have to pay attention to maintenance issues. What protection is there for all of you? Are you able to negotiate ground rules and honor them? Can you work with integrity and fairness, and display these qualities for each and every member of the group? Are you clear about the three-cornered contract you are in with the group and the organization, and the expectations of all concerned? How far can you be open with the group about your contract with their employer?

Considering all these questions will help you define your boundaries in working and, in turn, will allow you to work honestly and openly. Provide structure through theory or policy where necessary, but as a general rule, recognize the expertise that already exists in the group and allow others to diagnose the problem or make sense of the information. To use consultancy skills in facilitation, you must:

- use your self-awareness in the group as a basis for challenge and insight;

- have a style flexible enough to deal with a variety of people in any given situation; and

- be emotionally articulate so that you can help yourself and the group through difficult times.

Activity 61 Time Bandits

Facilitator Notes

This exercise is designed to raise awareness in groups about how they structure their time. The results, often surprising, may lead to increased productivity and certainly greater awareness about why things don't get done in meetings. The idea of "time structuring" comes from Eric Berne, founding father of Transactional Analysis, who believed that human beings are compelled to structure their time. He identified six patterns.

1. Introduce the following six structures of time. (5–10 minutes)

    Six Structures of Time:

    1. *Withdrawal* —not engaging, daydreaming, and being in our own world and thoughts
    2. *Rituals* —talking about the weather; making introductions; getting more tea or coffee
    3. *Pastimes* —talking about a topic but never moving to action (for example, "I remember when . . ." conversations or "Isn't it awful . . ." discussions)
    4. *Activities* —communication and behavior directed toward achieving a goal and undertaking some of the work that has to be done
    5. *Games* —communication with others that results in one person feeling confused or misunderstood; the desire to blame the other person in some way
    6. *Intimacy* —being honest about our thoughts and feelings in a given situation so that people feel we are being authentic with them (and not just spinning a line or saying what they want to hear)

2. Ask group members to reflect for a few minutes on how much time they spend in each so-called structure of time when they are in meetings. Ask them to estimate the percentage of overall time that they believe the team or group spends in each of the six structures. Ask participants to pair up or form small groups to see if there is any measure of agreement on how the group spends its time. Can they come up with any examples? What are their personal favorite ways of structuring their time? Do they think that the group as a whole has its own preferences? (10 minutes)

3. Draw the group back together and facilitate a discussion about meetings and time. How can we be more active and authentic in meetings? What blocks us? (10–15 minutes)

Note: As a facilitator, check how you spend your time in groups, too. For example, is there a tendency to want to pass time because you like hanging out with the group? Or are you a hard taskmaster, and thus minimize the time spent socializing or otherwise "off task"? How often do the groups you facilitate achieve intimacy? If they do, it is more likely that you are successfully employing consultancy skills in your work.

Activity 62 Conscious Intuition

Facilitator Notes

Use this exercise when you want to encourage people in your team or group to be more intuitive. Often, people have blocks against their own intuition, and many people mistakenly dismiss it as something that only women can access. In fact, it is a resource that we all share. We simply need to discover how to tap into it.

1. Ask group members to work in pairs with someone they do not know very well. Tell them that they are about to do an exercise that is about intuition, and that they need to focus for two minutes on their partner to try to get a real sense of who their partner is—without speaking. Ask them to think about what their partner's history might be, what interests they might have, whether they are more introvert or more extrovert, how content they are in their work, and what aspirations they might have. (2 minutes)

   Note: As the facilitator, you can expect some participants to be a little self-conscious or embarrassed at the start of this activity. Don't be put off by this. Tell participants it is normal to feel a bit awkward with people they don't know and somewhat self-conscious. It is part of the process.

2. After the 2 minutes are up, the pairs take turns telling (as they imagine it) each other's life story using their intuition and hunches.

   If there is resistance (that is, if people say they can't guess anything), encourage them to make something up to get them started. Once each person has told what they think is their partner's "life story," ask each pair to speak about the accuracy of the stories. (10–15 minutes)

3. The stories are often uncannily accurate, affirming the power of intuition. Draw the group back together and see what experience participants had. How do we access intuition? Do we trust it? How can we use it as facilitators? (15 minutes)

   The answer to this last question is that it can be used to make process observations about groups (for example, "I'm picking up that there's some underlying tension in the room. Does it have any meaning for the group?").

4. End this activity by asking participants to consider and discuss the following quote taken from Michael Gelb's book *Thinking for a Change*:

   "In the words of management genius Alfred Sloane, 'The final act of business judgment is intuitive.' Professor Weston Agor, author of *The Logic of Intuitive Decision Making*, discovered through extensive interviews that senior executives overwhelmingly pointed to a failure to heed their own intuition as the prime cause of their worst decisions.

   "In 1960, Ray Kroc's lawyers advised him against spending nearly $3 million on a couple of burger joints and the rights to the McDonald's name. Kroc stated that his 'funny bone' told him to overrule his counsel and make the deal."

   Ask participants:

   - What is this "funny bone"?
   - How can we bring more attention to our hunches? Should we do so?
   - Can we trust our gut? Why? Is all intuition body centered? (15 minutes)

Coaching

With your coachee, develop some of the skills of consultancy through role-play. First, discuss the skills of consultancy so that the coachee does not feel completely "at sea" for the next part of this exercise. Then run through the exercise so that the coachee can get a feel for the skills and identify those they should work on.

Present an organizational problem to the coachee and ask him or her to act as your consultant. Explore first of all what the problem presents in terms of mind, body, emotions, and spirit. Ask the coachee to think about the following questions:

- *Mind*—What is the coachee thinking about the issue you have presented (thoughts, theories, and principles)?

- *Body*—What physical sensations is the coachee experiencing? What is his or her gut telling the coachee? What does the heart desire?

- *Emotions*—What is the coachee feeling about the issue? Is it a juicy problem, or a dry old chestnut? Is it something you can work on with the coachee?

- *Spirit*—Using a metaphorical "third eye," what does the spirit's inner wisdom say about the problem? What are the beliefs involved, and what course of action would the higher self recommend?

Explore with your coachee how he or she felt about that exercise, and then go on to talk pragmatically about the problem you raised and what happened in reality. Use hindsight to develop thinking about what each party could have done better.

Facilitator Self-Development

1. It is important to understand your own motivations and needs that are being satisfied by being a facilitator. Work through the following questions, writing your answers in a journal so that you can reflect on them from time to time.

   This exercise is aimed at raising your self-awareness.

   - What do groups often not understand about you?
   - What are your favorite ways of structuring time in groups (see Activity 61)?
   - What roles or patterns do you find yourself in, even though you may want to change?
   - How much have you progressed in life and work that others don't realize, thus keeping you stuck?
   - What is it about facilitating groups that really turns you on?
   - What is your learning edge at the moment regarding groups?
   - Whom do you most admire as a facilitator/consultant? Why?
   - What would you love to say to the group you are currently working with (but dare not)?

3.6 Working in the Here and Now

So much of work is about "doing," about getting the job done, about achieving the task. There is nothing wrong with this, but the skillful facilitator has also learned how to be present, noticing what is going on in the here and now. This is where we make our best interventions.

An example helps to illustrate this issue: I once worked with a company as a facilitator. The agenda was team dynamics. I had been well briefed, and was introduced to several of the people I would be working with. It seemed a clear contract. From the moment I walked into the room, however, I was aware of a very subdued atmosphere. Thinking that maybe people would wake up once we got going, I started outlining the day and tried to engage the participants. There was little response.

I could have ignored the situation and ploughed on, but it is the facilitator's task to pay attention to energy, so I decided to check out what was going on. I told the participants what I was sensing and wondered aloud if they could explain it. After a period of silence, I was told that a number of people in the company had just been laid off. Not only were participants understandably shocked by this news, but they hadn't even been given the chance to say goodbye to their friends and colleagues because of the training.

Once I understood what was going on, I could empathize with the participants' situation and negotiate an agreement with them. What they needed was time at lunch to say a proper goodbye to their colleagues. Although the situation was far from ideal, by addressing the here and now issues, we were able to make the best of the rest of the day.

Working in the here and now requires acute awareness of what is happening at any given moment, listening to what people don't say and not being distracted by our own internal thoughts and opinions. Here are some useful points:

- When we are in "then and there" mode, we are dreaming of past or future situations, which have nothing to do with what is going on now. We are not attending to the present.

- When we are in "then and now" mode, our current behavior is being affected by our past experience. *In other words, our old patterns are being restimulated.*

- Being in "here and now" is where we want to be, but it's unrealistic to think we can achieve such attention all the time. We will sometimes drift off into the past or start imagining the future.

- Being "here and there" is equivalent to being empathetic and in full rapport with others—you are absorbed in their experience.

Being in the here and now is not always easy. We will get triggered by what other people say and do and we will sometimes get tired. Our attention will wander, and things from outside will sometimes distract us. But the more attention we can give to what is happening in the present, the better.

It is especially important to be comfortable in the present if you want to work with group process.

With process, there are no clear guidelines—it is an unpredictable world full of feelings and relationships, unconscious motivations, and ingrained behavior. It is also the place where teams and individuals frequently trip up and, consequently, stop being effective. When this occurs, it is essential that the facilitator be authentic and present, notice what is happening in the here and now, and stay with it.

Do not rush to find solutions and assume that what is emerging will be useful. By staying with the process, you are valuing people for who they are, modeling a way to manage feelings, and addressing what otherwise might sabotage the task.

As a facilitator, you need to be able to handle and highlight process issues, and resolve those that are obstructing the team from achieving its purpose. This means, as ever, that facilitators need to have already worked on their own self-development, experienced process, and understand how, by staying in the here and now, they can build self-awareness and create the conditions for changes in behavior.

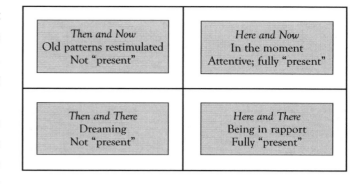

Activity 63 Multiple Personalities

Facilitator Notes

This is an exercise you might use with a team or group of trainee facilitators who are committed to their own development. Everyone adopts multiple roles or identities, and there will be different behaviors that accompany each of these. This activity helps participants identify their many identities, as well as identify a quieter and more receptive place within themselves.

1. In this paired exercise, Participant A has just one question to ask: "Who are you?" Participant B answers this question by talking about him- or herself. Participant A writes down the responses.

    For example, I might say when first asked this question: "I'm a facilitator, I'm a writer, I'm a father." When I've given my immediate answers, Participant A asks me the same question again. This time I respond with: "I'm a 40-year-old man, I'm a manager, I'm a coach." Again, when I run out of things to say, Participant A repeats the question. By this time I am running out of easy responses and will have to get more personal. "I'm a storyteller, I'm an exercise addict, I'm a traveler."

    Each time Participant B stops, Participant A asks again, "Who are you?" and it is Participant B's task to find an answer, to delve deeper, and to see what emerges. (5 minutes)

    Note: It is important that the pairs take time for this exercise. It is not to be rushed, and there are no prizes for coming up with the most identities. The purpose is to encourage Participant B to identify a number of these identities and see if he or she can find a quiet place within where the person beyond these identities resides!

2. Change over. (5 minutes)

3. Bring the team or group together and facilitate a discussion around the exercise.

    *   What was the quality of their experience?
    *   Was it easy or hard? If hard, what were the difficulties?
    *   Were people aware of all the identities that they described?
    *   Did people find a quieter place? How might that be relevant to facilitation? (10–15 minutes)

Activity 64 One-Word Snapshot

Facilitator Notes

At certain times, such as when the energy of the team or group is dispersed, it is useful to bring people back into the present with a short activity that highlights the thoughts, issues, or energy of the people involved. Try this exercise at the end of a session or at an appropriate time in the middle of a session when you think it would be helpful to give people a snapshot of where they are.

1. Ideally, participants should move into a circle (or at least into a position where all participants can see one another). Invite them to think of a word, a noise, or even a movement that best illustrates what they are feeling or thinking, or what is going on for them. If it is a word, make sure you write it on a flipchart so that this team or group energy is captured and can be reviewed the next time the team meets. (2–3 minutes)

2. Sometimes you will want to work with what emerges. At other times (such as at the end of a day), you won't want to process this information with the team or group. Let it stand for itself. Be sure to indicate that their work has value.

Activity 65 Attending

Facilitator Notes

Facilitators need to learn how to be "present" with others. This sounds easy, but it takes practice. This short activity highlights the skills you will need, as well as the ways in which we are all too easily distracted from what is happening right now.

1. Introduce the importance of being able to be in the present and pay attention. Highlight the skills required in free attention:
   - active listening skills
   - close observation of body language
   - tension-free attention
   - empathy
   - full awareness without internal chatter
   - being in the moment
   - free breathing
   - expectancy
   - benign intent
   - attuned to what might emerge
   - nonjudgmental (10–15 minutes)

(continued)

Activity 65 Attending *(concluded)*

2. Ask participants in the team to pair up and for Participant A to speak for 10 minutes about one of the following subjects: "last Christmas," "my last vacation," "my passion."

    As Participant A talks about this subject, it is Participant B's task to devote their complete attention to the speaker. B does not talk here. If Participant A dries up, then B simply waits until A starts again. As well as giving his or her best possible free attention, Participant B should notice what gets in the way of his or her giving free attention. Notice the chatter, the songs, the judgments, the distractions. (10 minutes)

3. At the end of the 10 minutes, invite the pairs to discuss what it was like to truly attend and what it was like to be on the receiving end. What did it feel like? How much effort was required in truly attending? How often do the recipients get this level of attention? Was it helpful? Would they like more of it? What got in the way for the people attending? (10 minutes)

4. Change over. (20 minutes)

5. Facilitate a discussion within the team or group about truly attending. Where would it be applicable in working situations (meetings, coaching sessions, conflict resolution)? What stops people from giving complete attention and receiving it? In a team, how do you know when the facilitator is truly attending?

    If you have time, practice giving "free attention" (as the facilitator), with the team discussing one of the topics above. Notice what it is like from the facilitator's and team's perspectives. Ask for feedback from all concerned. (10–15 minutes)

Coaching

This is an issue that focuses on what you are thinking and feeling moment by moment. When you are working with the coachee, you can help him or her by focusing on his or her self-awareness as well as on what happens to the coachee when he or she has meetings with clients and colleagues.

Ask your coachee to pay detailed attention to his or her thoughts, feelings, and body sensations. What does the coachee notice? And how will the coachee use the information that comes back? You may have to model real "presence" with your coachee, and perhaps get him or her to feel what it is like to have another person's complete attention (see Activity 65). Use yourself as a guinea pig, and let your coachee try to give you his or her complete attention. Then give the coachee feedback.

You can also explore with your coachee how to use this kind of "here and now" facilitation. When might it be useful with coachees, teams, or clients? When do you not use it? (When you don't want to deepen the process.) What are the risks of using it? (You may uncover more than you bargained for.)

Facilitator Self-Development

The following suggestions can help you build up your aptitude for working in the here and now:

1. Practice meditation or contemplation. In meditation, you will become far more aware of your own inner chatter and how it distracts you from the here and now.

2. The next time you are in a group or team meeting, notice the following:

   - How awake is the team or group?
   - How would you rate its energy on a scale of 1 to 10?
   - How would you describe its energy?
   - What distracts you from the here and now?

3. Join a therapy group, or attend a training course that deals specifically with group process.

3.7 Creative Facilitation

There is no doubt that we can all be creative (or at least more creative than we are used to being). But just how do we develop creativity? As facilitators, how can we foster creativity in our work with groups and teams?

There are, of course, a whole host of different approaches to boost creativity, but perhaps the most important attribute is to be open to new ideas. We may think that we are really seeing things as they are but, in truth, our past experience is a colored filter through which we constantly judge people and events. For example, how long does it take us to alter our opinion of someone if, on first meeting them, they make a bad impression? The answer depends on many factors, but the point here is that we limit ourselves and others when we have a fixed point of view. So creative thinking is about fostering openness. We can start to develop creative perception by engaging in activities that have been shown to promote playfulness, humor, and surprise.

- *Creative play.* One of the keys to creativity is to be able to loosen up our thinking and our framework of accepted behavior. Ask yourself how and when you play. Give yourself and group members permission to be silly with ideas and people, and notice how unrestricted or free you feel. Often it is the child within us who knows best how to play, and it is the child who knows how to look at things with a fresh mind.

- *Time for humor.* Often an outcome or an ingredient of play, humor seems to have no place in many professions. Yet when it comes to creativity, humor is essential. It encourages the absurd, the outlandish, and the irreverent, and helps us look at people and events in unlikely ways.

- *The artistic.* Creativity does not have to be an activity solely reserved for artists. However, our creative nature tends to get stifled at work. The challenge therefore is to find ways to unlock creative potential in whatever form that might take. Inviting groups to represent their thoughts and feelings through drama or art is a way of tapping into the less-used right side of the brain—the seat of creativity.

When we learn to work with the creative process, what we are really doing is learning to trust the creativity that is already within us. It is a simple enough idea, but it has immense implications. It means that we are already our greatest resource. We do not have to wait for someone else to stimulate us. We just have to get to know ourselves and the way we respond to the creative process.

Now this belief in "creativity for all" may be heartening, but those who are intent on displaying more creativity at work probably need to be reminded that they will face obstacles along the way. One such obstacle is the judgment that we often make about our own ideas; our inner critic can kill creativity before it starts to blossom. And if this isn't bad enough, other people can be hard to impress, too. For example, how many times have you seen group members propose innovative or unusual ideas, only to be put down by cynical managers? People who are working with creativity need to feel free to do things differently and to take risks. This does not mean that new ideas will escape being tested rigorously, but for creativity to flourish, you need an environment that is nonjudgmental and safe.

As facilitators, it is important to know how to draw out the creativity of the group when it is appropriate. Listening to your intuitive self will serve you and the group as a useful guide in deciding when and how to make those interventions. The skill is in being open yourself, and having the courage to try something new and different without being too attached to the outcome. When you adopt this attitude, the potential for feeling ridiculed, judged, or shamed as a result of your suggestion in the face of potential skepticism will be minimized. Try out ideas on friends first. Get support from allies who already work creatively in groups. Start with low ambitions and achievable goals, and build up to more risky strategies for creative processes.

Remember that we can all be greater than we allow ourselves to be, if only we are given the opportunity, and are nurtured and encouraged.

Activity 66 Creative Circle

Facilitator Notes

This is an exercise that uses neurolinguistic programming (NLP) principles to access and anchor resourceful and creative states for you or members of your group. If you don't know anything about NLP and want to find out more, try reading *NLP at Work* by Sue Knight.

1. This is a paired exercise. Each pair will need a briefing sheet (see below) so that they can talk their partners through the activity. Make sure that participants have enough space to move. (preparation time 5 minutes)

Briefing

You have 10 minutes to guide your partner through this exercise. Don't rush it. Encourage them to take their time as they go through the various stages. (10 minutes per person)

- Invite your partner to think of a creative experience they have had in the past when they felt resourceful, energized, and confident in what they were doing.
- Ask them to imagine a circle on the floor that is 3 yards in diameter and 1 yard in front of them. Ask them to visualize it and give it a color that will represent them at their most creative and resourceful moments.
- Ask them now to imagine being in the circle in that resourceful state:
  —What are they saying?
  —What are others saying?
  —What sounds and shapes are there?
- Ask your partner to explore fully everything that is happening in their mind's eye.
- Now ask them to step into the circle and re-live the feelings of the experience, allowing the feelings to build up as strongly as they like. Do they notice any physiological changes? If so, can they describe them? (For example, are they breathing more deeply, standing straighter, smiling, getting any feelings of warmth?) When they are satisfied, invite them to step out of the circle.
  Note: Observe in your partner any contrasts between stepping in and out of the circle regarding face color, breathing, muscles, balance, posture, eyes, and head position.
- Ask your partner to look at the circle again and see if there is anything they need to adjust.
- Ask them to step into the circle again. Is there anything they need to adjust from there?
- Finally, invite your partner to pick up that circle. Suggest that they can take it with them and repeat the experience again anytime, anyplace. Give them some time to complete and finish this exercise. Don't rush! (10 minutes per person)

(continued)

Activity 66 Creative Circle (*concluded*)

2. Make sure that both partners undertake this exercise. Once they have completed it, ask them to compare notes. What was their creative experience like? How easy was it to capture the detail in their imagination? In what circumstances might they be able to apply the creative circle? (10 minutes)

3. Bring the group back together and ask people to share any blocks to creativity they might have experienced, talk about any aspects of the exercise, and explain how this circle of creativity might help them. (10–15 minutes)

Note: This exercise can also be conducted as a whole-group exercise, with you reading out the instructions. The benefit of this is that you can control the pace and help participants who might feel a bit awkward about creativity to step into the process. Participants might feel silly doing it all together, but in a pair, they will have to take more responsibility for working through such feelings.

Activity 67 Bigger and Better

Facilitator Notes

The following exercises are about releasing creativity by tapping into humor. Use these exercises to energize and create flow when people feel stuck, or before any project that requires creative input.

In groups of three or four:

1. One participant makes a statement about something fantastic, unusual, or surprising that has happened to them. The next participant says: "that's nothing . . ." and then finds a more exaggerated story. See how far around the group can go before people have reached the stars, bought the moon, or met God. (5–10 minutes)

2. You might have seen this second activity in the past. We call it "Pompous Pontification." Participant A stands behind Participant B, who has his or her arms behind his or her back. A then hides behind B, but pushes his or her arms under B's armpits, and thus becomes B's arms. B pontificates about a subject (the project, him- or herself, a hobby), while A gesticulates in an exaggerated manner. Other group members are the audience. Switch roles. (3 minutes per pair)

3. Instruct each group to find methods of nonverbal communication to guide three people (sheep) across a room. The people are blindfolded, and the communicators (farmers) are not allowed to use words— only whistles, grunts, or claps. The course can include soft obstacles, but be careful! This exercise is excellent for team communication. Offer a prize.

Coaching

Using the following checklist, explore with your coachee any barriers that they may have to creativity. The stories that come out will give clues about barriers to creativity and signal work ahead that needs to be done.

Historical

- Any stories from childhood about your own creativity that you can recall.

Perception

- Are you able to see an issue from other points of view?
- Are you able to see a problem if it is not a problem for you?
- Are you too rigid or specific in how you define a problem?
- Do you put people into categories and make assumptions about them?

Emotion

- Are you afraid of failure, or are you willing to take risks?
- How do you deal with negative attitudes?
- How trusting are you?
- What happens when you are under additional pressure or strain?

Intellect

- Are you limited by a focus on logic and analysis?
- Do you rely too much on previous evaluations?
- Do you need more information?
- Is decision making difficult for you?

Expression

- How would you assess your communication skills?
- How do you translate ideas into words?
- Can you understand the ideas of others easily?

Cultural

- Does the organizational culture block you in any way?
- Do you follow the rules at all costs?
- Are you over-conscious of age, sex, religion, race?

Facilitator Self-Development

Try to include several of the following into your regular routines:

1. *Time alone.* Many people experience breakthroughs when they don't have people or deadlines pressing on them. Give yourself permission to take space for yourself, alone. Find a meditative exercise or activity and try not to have any expectations. You will soon find that the space you have created allows more of you to emerge.

2. *Dare to be different.* Go out with those people who have views that are different from yours, or ask for help from people who know nothing about the problem you are working on. Alternatively, put yourself in someone else's shoes and try to see the world from their perspective.

3. *Follow your bliss.* Look back at your life and find a time when you were at your best. What was going on for you at the time? Often these times are connected with a sense of inner freedom, so what are the opportunities for bringing some of those qualities into your life and work today?

4. *Mind, body, and emotions.* Take yourself seriously. Creativity isn't just stimulated imagination. Our creative expression usually flows best when we are in touch with all aspects of ourselves. Think of yourself as a whole system. Stretch your body and express your feelings as well as exercise your mind.

5. *Explore your inner world.* Personal development is all about discovering and challenging the way you operate in the world. Self-awareness is the first step on the path to change, and it is an essential ingredient if we want to start to flow more creatively. If you haven't started to look inside yourself, then it could be time to start.

6. *Practice creative thinking.* There are all sorts of creative techniques to discover, such as Mind Mapping, asking "what if" questions, making up paradoxical riddles such as "What is the sound of one hand clapping?" visualizing, and "becoming" the question.

7. *Keep a book for all those ideas, experiences, jokes, and quotes that you hear but usually forget.* You may also want to record your dreams—even if you can only remember snippets of their content. As you practice, you will remember more and more.

If this range of activities seems too daunting, bear in mind that they are only gateways to creativity. Choose the one that appeals to you most, practice it and see what happens. However, it is also worth remembering Edison's observation that creativity is "99 percent perspiration and 1 percent inspiration." We may have been lucky enough to have experienced the odd moment of enlightenment, but we shouldn't fall into the trap of thinking that creativity is either a predictable or a simple process.

3.8 Imaginal Work

The imaginal is a term used to incorporate a variety of techniques that are at the disposal of the facilitator and that help the team, group, or individual make sense of what is going on. Some of these techniques you will certainly know. For example, people often use metaphors to help illustrate the situation they are facing, such as "everything is rosy" or "we are a well-oiled machine." It is easy to see that such metaphors convey far more than simply stating "we are doing well."

Storytelling is another imaginal technique (see Activities 71 and 72) as are rituals, anecdotes, associations, analogies, imagery, and characterizations.

All the facilitators I know have their favorite imaginal techniques. Some like to drop in a piece of poetry every now and again or tell their pet anecdotes. Others like to engage participants in scenarios. You may be using some of these techniques already, but by consciously paying attention to those you wish to develop, you can build your skills and your range as a facilitator.

Why and How to Use the Imaginal

Some critics question the application and effectiveness of the imaginal. In a serious team meeting, for example, is it really appropriate to use these kinds of creative techniques?

It is particularly effective in such meetings, but the facilitator must be confident in using such techniques and reman objective about any intervention and its outcome.

In a tense team meeting, for example, a facilitator might use an image of team members "locking horns with each other" to try to illustrate what they see is happening. If the intervention is well timed and accurate, people within the team will pick it up and use it without further prompting.

One facilitator I know will often play-act as if he is choking himself when the team or group is stuck. His intent here is to physically enact or characterize what is happening between people in the room, and it often succeeds in moving the process along and giving people some insight into what is happening. But if it doesn't work or seems to go nowhere, this facilitator isn't overly concerned; after all, sometimes we get it exactly right, and sometimes we don't. The delight of using the imaginal, however, is that it is an invitation to the team or the individual to see things in a new light, to let creativity happen, and to be imaginative. This is true for facilitators themselves, as well as for the people with whom they are working.

One of the current themes in the workplace is how to help people bring more of themselves to work. The corporate poet David Whyte has been much in demand over the past few years for his ability to talk to leaders imaginatively about this dilemma. Is it really realistic, he challenges, to only want people to bring their positive qualities to work? If companies want to develop the full potential of their employees, they need to accept the whole person—their concerns and vulnerabilities, as well as their energy and enthusiasm. He suggests that it is rather like only being interested in the moon when it's waxing (but not when it's waning), and certainly not when it disappears from the sky.

There are echoes of this imagery in the story told by author and psychologist Robert Bly (*The Power of Shame*, New Dimensions Foundation, 1991), who suggests that employees come to work on Monday morning with a black bag around their waist into which they pack all the feelings and problems that they feel aren't acceptable at work. As the week goes by, he recounts, the bag gets heavier and heavier, dragging the employee down until it trips up other people and gets caught in the most inconvenient places.

As facilitators, we can borrow these metaphors and apply them to the learning situations we encounter. We can build our own store of useful teaching stories and we can offer our own imaginative associations, images, and memories to teams and coachees.

All this does require being prepared to take a risk—to share your own imaginal world with others. But this is a vivid and engaging way of working that brings facilitation and learning to life.

Activity 68 The Picture I Get

Facilitator Notes

This is an exercise that helps participants build up their confidence in using images as clarifying interventions. Although set up here as a one-to-one activity, the technique of using images can equally be applied to team or group situations.

1. Ask participants to pair up. Invite Participant A to speak for 5 to 10 minutes about a recent workplace problem that was difficult to resolve or was stressful. Ask Participant A to be as frank as possible about the people involved and his or her own part in the situation. (5–10 minutes)

2. It is participant B's task to listen actively and to see what associations or images they get about the situation that his or her partner is talking about. After A has spoken for a few minutes, it is Participant B's task to introduce the image or association that has come to mind.

   Example: Participant A has been talking about difficulties she has been having with a project team. It appears people aren't pulling together and are starting to blame one another for mistakes that have been made and deadlines that have been missed. She has held meetings, rescheduled the deadlines, and ensured that everyone is clear about their responsibilities and lines of communication. However, she is concerned that there is something she has missed.

   Participant B gets an image of something hidden in the shadow. After listening to A, B makes the following intervention: "The picture I get is that there's something lurking in the team that's just out of sight—something in the shadows. You can't see it clearly, but you are concerned it's going to appear later and affect the project."

3. After Participant B has introduced his or her image or association, the pair should continue for a minute or so to see if the intervention helps to clarify the situation or not. They should then consider the following questions:

   - Was the image accurate?
   - Did the intervention feel well timed and appropriate?
   - Did B feel attached to the intervention?
   - Was the intervention helpful? (5–10 minutes)

   Note: This is a practice exercise. It is vital that B not feel attached to his or her intervention. Sometimes it's when you don't get the intervention quite right that clarification then emerges (for example, Participant A responds to B's intervention, "No, it's not lurking, it's ready to pounce!"). Knowing that you don't always have to get it right takes the pressure off as well as helps keep you detached and objective.

4. Switch roles and repeat the exercise. (10–20 minutes)

Activity 69 The Moon

Facilitator Notes

This is an exercise based on metaphor to help participants focus on how much of themselves they bring to work.

1. Use the image of the cycle of the moon to discuss members of the team and the culture of the organization. Ask participants the following questions:

   • What qualities would you recognize as waxing qualities?
   • What qualities would you recognize as waning qualities?
   • What happens to people when they are in the space where there is no moon? (10–15 minutes)

2. Facilitate a group discussion. Is it right to expect that we bring the waning and "dark" sides of ourselves into work? Can we expect people to be alive and passionate at work if we only accept them when they are bright and sunny? (10–15 minutes)

Activity 70 Animals and Elements

Facilitator Notes

This is an activity that can help people on a team think of their roles and contributions in imaginative ways. It is drawn from the Native American tradition, and looks at the team as a whole entity that needs to have a balance of people with specific qualities.

The Model

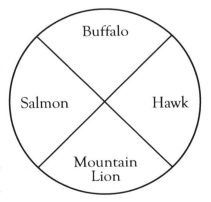

a. The Hawk represents the quality of Air.
   "Hawk" people have good planning and structural skills. They know where they are heading and how to get there. They know who are their allies and opponents. They also have a sense for the broader community and how to communicate with them. They have great vision.

b. The Mountain Lion represents the quality of Fire.
   Mountain Lion people have great energy, enthusiasm, and inspiration. They know what people get excited about and how to catch up on the latest gossip, skills, and information. They bring people into the team and make people feel good.

c. The Salmon represents the quality of Water.
   Salmon people understand what is going on in the depths and the currents of the team. They are sensitive to the team's feelings and its relationships. They know who likes whom, they are tuned in to the secrets of the team, and they know what hidden agendas are operating. They have a great sense for process.

(continued)

Activity 70 Animals and Elements (concluded)

d. The Buffalo represents the quality of Earth.

Buffalo people are nurturing, grounding, and practical. They keep the team in touch with what is realistic. They are also very safe, reliable, and strong. They appreciate the team's resources and understand the team's limitations, and are excellent at reaching their goal.

1. Create a handout of the model on the previous page and distribute a copy of it to each participant to consider their own qualities. Ask them to color in the quadrant that best represents the quality that they believe is strongest in them. (10 minutes)

2. Invite participants to pair up and to consider with their partner the following questions:

   - Where are they strongest?
   - Where are they weakest?
   - What quality would they most like that they don't have?
   - Who do they get along with best on the team? What qualities do they see that person as having—the same as them, or different?
   - Does their partner see them in the same way? (10 minutes)

3. Place all the models on the floor in a circle or stick them up on the wall, and consider the makeup of the whole team. Does it have a balance of people with different qualities? If not, is that a problem? (5–10 minutes)

4. Participants might question the accuracy of the self-assessment. If so, draw a large model on a flipchart and invite the team to determine the qualities of each individual on the team. For each participant, color in a section of the quadrant that best represents their quality. If the team decides that someone has a balance of qualities, they can put color in more than one quadrant. At the end of this activity, there will be a team assessment.

   Again, assess with the team whether or not the balance is right, and where its weaknesses lie. (15–20 minutes)

Coaching

The best way to teach the imaginal is to model it yourself and to consider with your coachee how people can be encouraged to be more innovative and creative at work.

Within your one-to-one sessions, see if you can encourage your coachee to think of his or her team or situation in new ways. Use creative interventions, such as metaphors. Alternatively, drop into the sessions some of your own inspirations or anecdotes. Here are a few to help you on your way:

Come to the edge. We might fall. Come to the edge. It's too high. Come to the edge. And they came, and he pushed and they flew. Christopher Logue.

If at first the idea is not absurd, then there is no hope for it. Albert Einstein.

We don't see things as they are. We see things as we are. Anais Nin.

Everything that irritates us about others can lead us to an understanding of ourselves. Carl Jung.

There is no limit to what a man can achieve, as long as he doesn't care who gets the credit. Bob Woodruff.

Facilitator Self-Development

If you are going to use imaginal techniques, you will want to find those with which you are most comfortable. The following suggestions can help you explore your imaginal style:

1. Become aware of metaphors and how you might use them. Think of a metaphor for your company, your job, your boss, your team, the places where you feel most uncomfortable, a time of great change.

2. Check out a relaxation CD from your library on which there is a guided visualization.

3. Consider joining a local theatre group or participating in training about how theatre-based techniques can be used in business. Find out more from Praxis (Shakespeare), Actors in Business (presentation), and Action in Management (role-plays and theatre techniques).

4. If you have children, make up an adventure story with them. Try not to plan it, but trust your imagination and see where it leads you.

3.9 Using Stories to Facilitate Learning

Stories! What relevance do they have to training and development? Surely stories don't belong to the world of business!

If this is your view, it may be time to think again. If you are a manager, trainer, facilitator, or coach, you know that sometimes you have to engage others in ways that bridge old divisions or that unexpectedly illuminate new paths. Stories can do this, and if you have access to the right story at the right time, you have a powerful resource at hand.

You may be familiar with training films, which are often based on the telling of a story. Take, for example, *Does The Team Work?* the Video Arts film that focuses on the plight of the space freighter Nostradamus. Even before we hear about the details, we are taken into another world that promises to give us a new perspective on the complex behaviors and mysterious events that occur in life. In this respect, it is a metaphor, helping us to make sense of the world and our part in it.

Myths, too, are metaphors. They are fantastic stories, but they also carry profound truths that resonate with us and relate to the challenges we face today. David Whyte, for example, has written about the classic hero Beowulf and his fight against the monster Grendel. Whyte suggests that it is the role of the warrior to challenge the monster. In this story, however, the monster isn't defeated; instead, it escapes back into a dark lake.

But who dares to follow the monster into his lair? And what awaits us in the unknown waters?

This myth resonates for many people who are faced with daunting tasks and the requirement to step into the unknown. But when faced with the dark lake, do we dare to change? What danger lurks beneath the water? Will we survive?

Such stories provide us with maps of the inner psyche. They are psychologically valid and emotionally realistic, even when they seem to be fantastic, impossible, or unreal. The fact that such stories have lasted for thousands of years also supports the notion that they speak to people about their personal and interpersonal challenges as powerfully today as at any time in the past.

So how can storytelling work on a more everyday level for trainers and developers?

Experience suggests that it is important for trainers to know their story well and to know when to use it. This means that the trainer should not be too attached to the story itself. It is worth remembering that when told at the wrong time or to the wrong audience, a story may be off-putting. On the other hand, the right story at the right time can add tremendous depth to a learning event or intervention. In other words, the story needs to be relevant and timely. If you are planning to use a story, make sure you know it well, that it is succinct, that it can be explained, and that you know what your intention is in telling it. Does it illustrate something about the group process? The culture of the company? Power games in the organization? Or does it enlighten thinking on a particular situation, or teach something about behavior or feelings?

There are two main approaches to storytelling that trainers need to consider.

The first is to develop your own archive of stories that you think are appropriate for learning situations. Whether you are interested in myth or more contemporary tales, make sure you have a range of stories to draw from that you feel can help others.

The second approach is to draw from the participants themselves. Many people will have ries that they want to tell: "real" stories of people they've known or fictional stories that have a deep meaning for them. The issue for trainers here, however, is to keep learning in mind: people may be very attached to their own stories, but if you are using their material, focus it on the issue at hand, or you will quickly lose your way and your audience's attention.

The real invitation with storytelling, however, is to embrace creativity and be prepared to take a risk. Look into stories that speak to you. Try out short stories with audiences and gauge their reaction. Most important of all, try to understand what it is that draws you to the stories you want to tell to others.

Activity 71 The Golden Fleece

Facilitator Notes

Every team will, at some stage, become demotivated, discouraged, or feel stuck. This activity is for facilitators or managers who want to help a team understand its "process," its obstacles, and its diversity.

1. Introduce the idea of stories as metaphors (see theory) and suggest that you are going to use the well-known story of Jason and the Argonauts as a framework to understand where you are as a team. You may need to research it a little. Tell the team the basic story line. (10–15 minutes)

   In order to win his throne, Jason has been given the impossible task by his uncle, the king, of fetching the golden fleece from the distant island of Colchis. The king hopes it will be the last he sees of Jason. However, with the support of Hera, queen of the Gods, Jason accepts the challenge and sends a herald to call for the ablest heroes in the land to accompany him on the quest. Many came, but only 50 were chosen, including Hercules (for his strength), Theseus (for his valor), Orpheus (for his music), Zetes and Calais (the sons of the North Wind), Mosus (who could speak to the birds), Idmon (the prophet), and Ancaios (the astrologer). They became known as the Argonauts after their ship, the Argo.

   On the journey, however, there were many dangers. On Lemnos, the first island they anchored at, they were seduced by the local women, and would have stayed there if Hercules had not dragged them back to the ship. On another island, they were attacked in the middle of the night by monsters, and inadvertently killed their host in the confusion. On a third island, water nymphs seized Hercules' squire, Hylas. Hercules then left the company to look for him. On a fourth island, a king challenged one of the Argonauts to a boxing match; but when the king had been defeated, the Argonauts had to run for their lives from the furious islanders. Additionally, they had to deal with harpies, clashing rocks, fever, and wild animals before reaching King Aietes in the land of Colchis.

   With the help of the king's daughter, Medea, Jason manages to steal the golden fleece. There are still many dangers to negotiate, and it is many years before he is able to return to Iolcus to claim his throne. As an old man, Jason dies while sitting in the shadow of the Argo dreaming of the adventures of his youth.

2. Divide the team into pairs and ask them to discuss their team as modern-day Argonauts. What was their vision? What skills did they bring? What were the selection tests? What were their feelings at being chosen? (10–15 minutes)

3. Ask the whole team to identify the main characters in their journey—both friends and foes. See if the team can identify the roles of these characters (friendly or unfriendly kings, tricksters, harpies, seducers, and so on). Ask them to think about the conditions of the journey (e.g., stormy, becalmed, marooned). Ask one of the team members to facilitate this meeting. See what emerges. Encourage the team to think metaphorically. (15–20 minutes)

4. Now ask another team member to list on a flipchart the skills, resources, and aid they have needed to get past their difficulties. Who has been called upon during the journey, and what qualities did they show? Have they lost anyone along the way? Has that person been remembered? If so, how? (15–20 minutes)

(continued)

Activity 71 The Golden Fleece (concluded)

5. Map the journey. Ask the team to think of an invisible axis stretching across the room. Ask them to imagine that their starting point is at one end of the room and the fleece is at the other. Then ask them all to place themselves somewhere between those end points, depending on how far away they perceive the golden fleece to be. This part of the exercise will manifest what people feel about the team's progress. Did they feel close to, or far away from their goal? It will also show who is most discouraged, pessimistic, or in need of help. Be prepared to acknowledge feelings and challenge perceptions. (10–15 minutes)

6. Whatever the real or imagined progress, this exercise provides the manager/facilitator with the opportunity to acknowledge the team's achievements and to reinforce the point that the process of working together can be as important as the final objective (which, even when it is reached, might itself just be another staging post on a longer journey). Help the team come up with suggestions about how it can recognize its successes, enjoy its progress, and support itself on an ongoing basis. (15–20 minutes)

Activity 72 Heroes and Villains

Facilitator Notes

This is an activity that could be run by a trainer who wants to help facilitators or managers understand the use and place of storytelling in organizations. It is also useful for managers who want to help their teams raise their awareness about culturally acceptable or unacceptable behavior, and define what constitutes good performance.

1. Explain to participants why you are proposing this creative exercise (see above). Outline its structure and tell participants that you are going to start off looking generally at heroes and villains. You will then be focusing on the relevance this issue has for people and teams. (5 minutes)

2. To start with, ask the group to identify some popular real-life heroes and villains. (*Note:* Some people's heroes will be other people's villains.) (5 minutes)

3. The emphasis is on "winning" and "star" performance, a concept that is appropriate to many teams and businesses. Ask participants, "So what are the characteristics that you, your colleagues, and your managers expect to see in a 'heroic' employee?" Some of the qualities that might be raised are: dazzling intellect, courage, resilience, brilliant interpersonal skills, great humor, innovative ideas, a rebellious streak.

   Then focus on the villain and ask, "In the same vein, how do we recognize the traits of villainy?" For example, disloyalty, laziness, untrustworthiness, self-serving, one-upmanship, lying. (10 minutes)

4. Now ask participants to try to remember one occasion when they were cast as a "hero" at work, and one time when they have been cast as a "villain." (These experiences do not have to be dramatic.) Ask participants to note down the facts of the situation. (10 minutes)

(continued)

Activity 72 Heroes and Villains (concluded)

5. Divide the group or team into pairs. In turn, each member of the pair is asked to relate his or her story. The partner-listener then prompts the speaker with the following questions:

   - What was the role of other people in these events? (Was there an adversary, a trickster, a friend, a guide, an ally?)
   - What were the consequences of these events?
   - Was your success or villainy recognized?
   - How long did the repercussions last?
   - How did other people react?
   - What lessons did you learn? (20 minutes)

6. Bring the group back together and ask for volunteers to share their stories with the group. What has emerged? What is the common experience? Draw out from the group how, in their experience

   - Heroes become heroes. Are such people gifted? Lucky? Favored or helped? Risk-takers? Are successes taken for granted? Envied? Valued? How does the team/organization recognize its heroes?
   - Villains become villains. Can villains be successful? Are mistakes covered up? Are people forgiven? Is there a learning culture? Is failure tolerated?

Draw the session together. What have people learned? What are the weaknesses and strengths of the current organization?

Coaching

Everyone has a story to tell. When you are coaching, you can drop in your own stories to illustrate the technique, but you should also encourage your coachee to tell his or her own stories. What was his or her career journey to this company? What anecdotes does the coachee have to tell?

Encourage your coachee to structure a story (about the time the team succeeded beyond expectations, or about something that the coachee did in his or her personal life that helped him or her learn an important lesson) to tell you.

Part of storytelling is about daring to take a risk, so be prepared to run a story-swapping session. If your coachee wants some good material to draw from, encourage him or her to read up on how we can bring our passion and soul into work.

One of the real dangers of storytelling is that we become too attached to a particular tale, so it is important to work with the coachee on his or her story. Why is it important to them? What are the messages that are coded within it? Can the coachee offer it and be prepared for people to discard it as something irrelevant or even worthless? Or is it too "precious" to him or her to share it?

Facilitator Self-Development

With storytelling, one of the key themes for your own development is delight. What stories do you most like to hear? What captures your imagination? You have to give yourself room to be enchanted. You don't have to give up your adult mind, but try to bring out the part of you that can dream and fantasize.

The following suggestions can help you explore storytelling:

1. Become aware of metaphors and how you might use them. Think of a metaphor for your company, your job, your boss, your team, the places where you feel most uncomfortable, a time of great change.

2. If you have young children or grandchildren, nephews or nieces, practice on them. Find children's stories that you like, memorize them, and tell them. Alternatively, make up your own stories as you go along. Don't worry if you get stuck—you can always ask your audience to think about what might happen next.

3. Keep a notebook of the stories you hear that capture your attention and that you think could be useful in learning situations. Shakespeare's works teach people about leadership through stories such as *Julius Caesar* and *A Winter's Tale*. Legends such as that of Jason and the Argonauts can help us think in new ways about team development. What are the themes that you are working on with people, and what stories might be useful to you?

3.10 Endings

Endings in groups need attention and management, as they tend to arouse strong feelings and anxieties. For this reason, endings are often ignored. To keep emotions at bay, sometimes groups pretend that endings are not happening or that they are not important.

This may all sound a little melodramatic— I mean, we're talking about the world of work here, aren't we? This is true, but even in brief meetings, we tend to return to the patterns of behavior we learned in the past. Some facilitators always run out of time for an ending and ignore it completely; others can't quite find a way to say goodbye. Then there are those who are always trying to make plans for next time as the team or group leave the room.

It is not only facilitators who find endings difficult. Just consider your old school groups. To avoid saying goodbye, these kinds of groups will often arrange a reunion, but when the day arrives, only half the group shows up. The reason for the reunion planning has more to do with denial that the "group" is finished as such, rather than the relationships people have or don't have with one another.

One of the problems facilitators encounter with endings is that people either take them too seriously, or don't take them seriously enough. Everyone has their own pattern of behavior when it comes to endings, which creates competing tensions in the group. You'll recognize many of these behaviors:

- *premature leaving* of the group or meeting
- *withdrawal,* demonstrated by lateness or disengagement

- *being distracted* by the future and what to do next, rather than staying with the here and now
- *anger,* for example, because of an argument either with the leaders or with another group member
- *disappointment* if the experience has been good and members feel supported by the group
- *resentment* if unfinished business has not been attended to during the life of the group

These are all avoidance behaviors that the facilitator must handle with sensitivity and awareness. Bear in mind, too, that a sense of achievement is crucial to a good ending, because feelings of inadequacy, failure, and anger will be generated if there is not a sense of task completion.

Endings are important even when a group or meeting has been difficult, as they allow the overall experience and learning to be reviewed and evaluated. Through this evaluation, members can then move on psychologically and emotionally, taking their personal and professional learning into the future. Well-observed endings thus become a clearing process for the old and an opportunity to integrate new learning and development.

Help people disengage by time-structuring the agenda so that everyone knows when and how the ending will happen. Endings can include the following:

- a summary of main points
- action planning
- an opportunity to discuss any other business
- an agreement as to the time of the next meeting
- sticking to time boundaries
- formal closure of the meeting (usually by thanking everyone for their time)

For training events or longer-term group programs, endings are typically achieved through

- an evaluation of the learning or task achievement;
- members sharing openly about how they feel about endings;
- a ritualistic marker of the end, such as a certificate awarded, a meal together, or an ending exercise;
- action planning; or
- self- and peer-assessment.

Whatever you do, be sure to leave enough time for the ending. Be aware of your own pattern of ending, and share the information to highlight the richness of endings for the group and model how patterns of behavior can become part of the facilitator's style. Make sure that you end intentionally; that is, contract with the group that there will be time for endings, and stick to this agreement. However, don't be surprised if you notice a whole range of contradictory feelings emerging; these may feel stormy, but it is likely that they will have nothing to do with you. They are normal behaviors to be expected when people are saying goodbye.

Activity 73 Self- and Peer-Assessment

Facilitator Notes

This is a powerful ending, ideal for short training programs and long-term groups. It helps people reflect on what they have learned and practice giving and receiving feedback.

Note: It is important to keep clear time limits; otherwise, this exercise can get bogged down. There may also be a lot of anxiety, so keep the momentum moving and make sure that there is a balance of positive and constructive feedback. Leave time at the end of this exercise in case there needs to be any debriefing or additional input from you.

1. Mention at the beginning of the course or group that there will be some self- and peer-assessment at the end of the course to highlight what has been learned and to identify any gaps in learning that may need to be addressed. This establishes the understanding that learning is a continuous process and will help participants focus on their own learning and development. It would be useful to offer the group some guidelines on giving feedback and receiving feedback (see Section 1.10) before doing this exercise.

2. At the end of the course, leave 20 minutes for participants to reflect on

   • what they have learned and what they still have to learn; as well as
   • the strengths and learning needs of others in the group.

3. Allow 10 minutes per participant for the self- and peer-assessment process, which will include the following:

   • a 5-minute self-assessment statement by each participant, based on his or her perceived skill levels, confidence levels, perceived strengths and weaknesses, and what he or she may still need to learn
   • concise feedback from other members of the team or group on their strengths and learning needs.

   Bear in mind any agreed-upon rules of feedback.

   If the group you are working with is large, divide it into two or three smaller groups for the purposes of the exercise. Remember that it is easier for people to give more detailed feedback in a smaller, more intimate group than in a large one.

4. Add your own feedback as a completion of the exercise.

Activity 74 Five W-H

Facilitator Notes

This is a practical, action-plan-focused ending approach that can be used for short courses. Adapt it for use in meetings where learning has been part of the agenda.

1. Invite group members to reflect on their experiences, and think about how they can put the new learning to practical use.

   - What learning do you want to apply?
   - With whom?
   - Where?
   - When?
   - Why? What do you hope to achieve?
   - How will you do this so that it is best for all concerned?

2. Ask people to form small groups to discuss their reflections, or ask people to state their reflections in the whole group to give it additional emphasis.

Activity 75 Cutting the Ties

Facilitator Notes

This is a ritualistic ending for a longer-term group or, for example, a cross-functional project team. There must first be a level of trust, since it illuminates the network of relationships that form over the process of a group. This can make it a powerful ending exercise. (10–20 minutes)

Materials: You will need a ball of string and a pair of scissors.

1. Ask for a volunteer to start the ending process and go over the following:

   Whoever volunteers first takes the ball of string and wraps one end securely around one finger of their non-dominant hand. They are to make eye contact with someone they feel they have connected with or learned from during the course. They then throw or pass the ball of string to this person. At this time, they can say (briefly and specifically) what it is they appreciate about that person.

2. The person who receives the ball of string does not respond to what is said. Instead, he or she wraps the string around their finger and throws or passes it to someone else, making an appreciative statement.

3. This is repeated until the string is used up and a web of connections has been created in the space between group members, linking each member by the threads on their fingers.

4. The facilitator then picks up a pair of scissors (which have been left close by), and slowly and silently cuts the string a few inches away from their own fingers and passes the scissors on so that everyone does the same. This signifies the end.

Activity 76 Group Gifts

Facilitator Notes

This is an ending that encourages people to consider one another in the context of the group and make some real contact with one another, giving one another the gift of appreciation. (15–20 minutes)

1. This exercise starts with you, the facilitator: Tape a blank sheet of paper onto each participant's back.

2. You then invite each participant to walk around and to write on each person's paper the one quality that they have seen most clearly in that person OR jot down the "gift" that they would most like to give to that person.

3. At the end of the exercise, ask each participant to take a turn reading aloud those qualities or gifts that people have written on their sheet of paper.

Coaching

When you are nearing the end of a coaching session, it is crucial that you review the contract with the coachee and see how far you have traveled in achieving the goals identified. It is important for the coachee to have room to say what he or she has learned; what he or she has implemented; any changes in behavior, attitudes, or skills; and what he or she liked and did not like about the sessions. The coachee should thoroughly evaluate what he or she has learned, achieved, and still has left to do in the future, with or without the coach's support.

It is also important for the coachee to give you specific feedback on how you helped him or her as well as feedback on the things you did that did not seem helpful to him or her. Encouraging this will show that you are recognizing growth as a continuous process.

Discuss your relationship and what form it will take from now on. For example, will you still meet occasionally or keep in touch in some other way? Give feedback to the coachee from your perspective about what you have learned from them; after all, the learning process is never one way!

Decide what to do together to mark the end. Will you undertake a ritual together (such as having a drink)? Or will it be a quick goodbye as you move on to the next meeting? What will be the pattern of your joint ending? This, of course, will be heavily influenced by the pattern of your individual endings. These may be worth sharing so that each of you has an understanding of the other's ending behavior.

Facilitator Self-Development

Discover your own individual pattern of ending by reflecting on the following:

1. How do you end courses, jobs, meetings? Do you ignore the end and act as if nothing ever really ends as long as you know how to contact people? Do you labor the end and begin to dwell on it prematurely? Or do you give the end due recognition and credit, without minimizing its significance or becoming overly emotional?

(continued)

Facilitator Self-Development (*concluded*)

2. How you end personal relationships will give you clues to your own pattern of ending. For example, some people have a string of ex-partners as friends because they cannot end a relationship. Think about what you tend to do.

3. Your cultural background may have influenced your ending patterns. I come from a tradition of Yorkshire grit, and remember being told at the age of 10 not to cry at my grandfather's funeral because I would set everyone off! Sometimes the messages we receive as a child support our patterns of ending in adulthood. Think about how your cultural tradition influences your ending patterns now.

4. What does all this mean for your facilitation style on endings? What do you need to do to achieve healthy endings in groups that you run?

Made in the USA
Lexington, KY
02 November 2016